Good Apple and Seasonal Arts and Crafts

Written and illustrated by
Nancee McClure

Cover by Kathryn Hyndman

Copyright © Good Apple, Inc., 1990 Revised

ISBN No. 0-86653-087-8

Printing No. 987654321

Good Apple, Inc.
1204 Buchanan St., Box 299
Carthage, IL 62321

Table of Contents

INTRODUCTION

In times past, the calendar determined much of what people did during the course of their lifetimes. Waking, sleeping, planting, harvesting, working and celebrating were all determined by where the sun was in the sky. All of the modern conveniences which have protected us from the elements have also, to a certain degree, alienated us from them. This book was designed to provide projects for an art program that will help keep the students in harmony with the changes in the seasons.

Special emphasis has been given to the major holidays. These events are usually so important in grade school children's lives that they can be used to stimulate and focus on activities that will aid in developing the children's aesthetic discrimination.

Somewhere around the third grade children change their attitudes about expressing themselves artistically. Younger children approach art projects with free abandon, and the process seems to be more important to them than the end product. The new social awareness of third or fourth graders can tend to make them dissatisfied with their projects and critical of the end results. Since drawing and painting are areas in which the end results can look the most immature, this is a perfect time of life for children to be introduced to craft projects. A constructing activity will be "safer" because the end results are more predictable.

This is also an age when the teacher needn't be overly concerned with originality in art projects, or "copying." If one child's drawing in the room looks just like someone elses, it just means that he is unable to deal with "uncharted territory." The child may not be ready to create something personally original until he/she has seen it explored by someone else.

The majority of the craft projects in this book use supplies that would be readily available to any classroom teacher. Assuming that most school districts have little money left over for the art program nowadays, most of these supplies could be gotten for free or saved by teachers and cooperative parents. Paper can be gotten from printers and paper companies, wood scraps from lumber yards, plastic containers and styrofoam trays from the butcher,

1

and so on. Here is a list of things to save or scrounge that can come in really handy:

wood scraps	egg cartons
driftwood	carpet scraps
milk cartons	gunny sacks
plastic milk jugs	fabric scraps
plastic detergent bottles	yarn scraps
margarine tubs	string
grocery sacks	styrofoam meat trays
cardboard tubes	boxes
newspapers	coat hangers
wallpaper sample books	cardboard
paint sample cards	empty thread spools
egg and fruit separators	sticks and dowels
magazines	telephone wire
Popsicle sticks	tongue depressors
clothespins	buttons and beads
pop top rings	six-pack plastic

Ideas for activities and projects can come from all kinds of resources. Below is a list of a few free (or almost free) booklets and pamphlets containing arts and crafts activities.

A Raft of Crafts Send to Johnson Wax, Dept. WWC, Golden Rondelle, P.O. Box 567, Racine, Wisconsin (projects using throwaways)

Move Over Michaelangelo Send to Church & Dwight Company, 2 Pennsylvania Plaza, New York, New York (making and molding homemade clay)

Beautiful Junk Send to U.S. Dept. of Health, Education and Welfare, Office of Child Development, Washington, D.C. 20201 Ask for #73-1036. (sources for free materials)

Patterns for Miniature Furniture Send 50 cents to Green Door Studio, Dept. W, 517 E. Annapolis St., St. Paul, Minnesota 55118 (patterns for 50 pieces of miniature furniture)

Pit-Niks Make History Send to Pit-Niks, P.O. Box 2162, Costa Mesa, California 92626 (things to make from avocado pits)

Softy's Craftbook Send to Q-TIPS, P.O. Box 4030, Jefferson City, Missouri 65101 (constructions and art projects for parents, teachers and kids)

Thanks to Lenore McClure for many of the ideas used in this book.

September

Arts & Crafts
School Spirit Banner

Cheer your team on with colorful pennants!

Supplies: One piece of felt or fabric cut to a 9" x 22" diamond per student. (Choose one of your school colors.)

Plenty of fabric or felt scraps from which the students can cut school letters, slogans or emblems

One-quarter-inch dowel (36" long) per student

Paper to cut patterns

Pins, needles, thread, glue, rulers, scissors

Procedure: Cut a few patterns of 9" x 22" isosceles triangles for your students to use. At this time also cut some patterns measuring 9" x 2" and 6" x 1". These will be used to fold over the end of the pennant and attach to the pennant base. (See illustration.) Assemble the pennants by using the patterns to cut your fabric. Fold the 9" x 2" strip in half lengthwise and pin it to the end of the banner. Sew it into place. Cut "v" shaped cuts into the ends of the 6" x 1" strips and fold them as shown. Stitch into place. Draw outlines of school emblems and letters on paper. Use these as pattern pieces and cut the fabric accordingly. Glue them into place. Thread the dowel through the opening and cheer your team to victory!

Name Designs

Supplies: Construction paper
Glue, scissors, pencil
Crayons

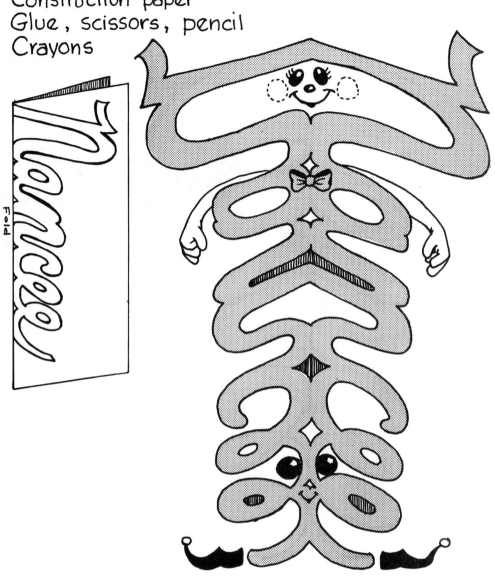

Procedure: Start out with a 9"x 12" piece of colored construction paper. Fold the paper lengthwise and write your name on it as shown in the smaller sketch above. Writing your name a couple of times with crayon will give the lines enough thickness to cut on both sides of the letters. Cut on both sides of the crayoned line making sure that the name is held together on the fold. Glue the name on a contrasting colored piece of construction paper. Add additional details with cut pieces of construction paper to suggest an image.

Pencil 'n Pen Holder

Supplies: 1-quart plastic bottles (1 for each student)
Scissors
Yarn (about 13 yards per student)

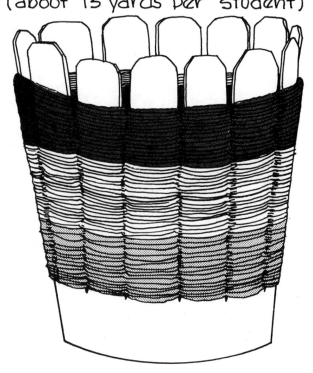

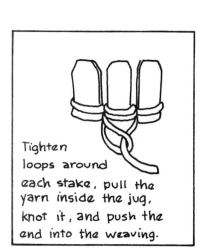

Tighten loops around each stake, pull the yarn inside the jug, knot it, and push the end into the weaving.

Procedure: Cut the neck and shoulders off the plastic bottle so it's about 6 or 7 inches tall. Then cut sections to about 1½ inches from the bottom of the jug. You will need to cut an odd number of sections, and the finished piece will look better if the sections are even. A good way to achieve this is to cut a piece of yarn the size of the circumference of the jug; then measure it and divide it into 11 or 13 equal sections. (Don't cut it, just mark it.) Wrap it back around the jug and mark the jug where you should make your cuts. Now, beginning with the inside bottom, begin to weave the yarn over and under. When you wish to change colors, tie the two pieces of yarn in a knot and continue to weave. To finish it off, loop the yarn around each stake in the top row (see sketch above).

Fall Leaf Collage

Supplies: Several different kinds of fresh leaves
Different colors and textures of paper: manilla,
    parchment, paper bag, newsprint, etc.
A sturdy piece of cardboard for a backing
Brown or black construction paper
Water soluble block printing ink and a brayer
Scissors, rubber cement

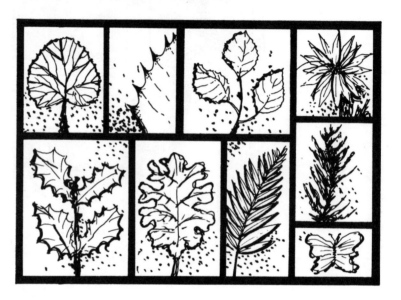

Procedure: You should have at least ten different objects
to print. Using the water soluble block
printing ink, make at least twenty small prints,
using different colors of ink and several different
colors and textures of paper. When the prints
are dry, choose the 10-12 best ones and
trim them. Experiment with different arrange-
ments and when one is satisfactory, rubber
cement the prints onto the cardboard backing. (You may have to trim the cardboard to
suit your arrangement.) Take strips of brown
or black construction paper and rubber cement
border trim around the prints. As a finishing
touch, a little bit of spatter painting will add
an antique, textured look to the prints.

Patchwork Patterns

Supplies: White paper, cut in squares (whatever size is convenient, but at least 8" x 8")
Black and colored markers
Crayons, rulers, compasses
Colored paper and/or fabric scraps
Scissors, glue

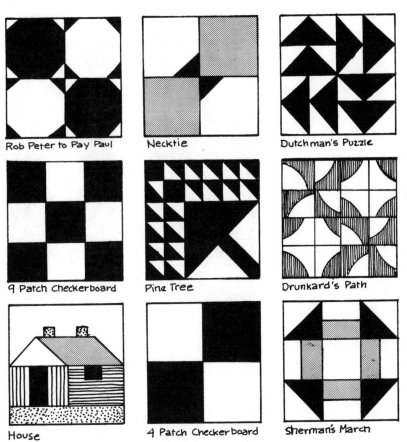

Rob Peter to Pay Paul   Necktie   Dutchman's Puzzle

9 Patch Checkerboard   Pine Tree   Drunkard's Path

House   4 Patch Checkerboard   Sherman's March

Procedure: Here's a good chance for your students to learn about the traditional craft of patchwork. Pass out the plain white squares and show the kids some traditional patterns like the ones shown above. Have them create their own patterns using geometric designs. Then have them create names for their designs. When all the students are finished, put them up together on a wall in the classroom.

Note to the Teacher: Encourage the students to use patterns in their patchwork designs: stripes, polka dots, paisleys. This will make the end result brighter and more interesting.

Seed Mosaics

Supplies: Sturdy pieces of cardboard for backing
All kinds of seeds and dried beans and peas
Fabric dye (if you should want to dye some of them)
White glue
Toothpicks

Procedure: If you want to dye some seeds, dissolve one teaspoon of powdered dye in ½ cup of hot water. Bring the solution to a boil and remove it from the heat. Drop a small amount of seed in and stir for a minute, then spoon the seeds out and let them dry on several layers of paper towels. To make the seed mosaic, draw the basic design on the piece of cardboard. Working with one small area at a time, spread the glue on and then carefully put the seeds of your choice down. Push the seeds as close together as you can with a toothpick. Some seeds may be overlapped or glued up on end for variety. When the mosaic is completed brush several layers of diluted glue over the seeds.

Found Object Sandcast

Supplies: Found objects: acorns, nuts, shells, machine
parts, or any interestingly shaped small
objects.
Sand
Plaster of Paris
Sturdy cardboard boxes or gallon milk jugs
with the tops cut off (1 for each student)
An empty spray bottle you can fill with water

If you want to hang
your sandcast later,
epoxy glue a looped
wire to the back.

Procedure: Fill your carton or box with 3-4 inches of
sand. Using the spray bottle, dampen the sand
well with water. Stamp the found objects
firmly into the sand in a pleasing design.
After the impressions have been made, gently
remove the objects. Some small objects may
be left in the sand (like bits of colored glass,
buttons, etc.) to be imbedded into the plaster
cast. In an old bucket or wastepaper basket,
mix the plaster according to the directions on
the package. Pour the liquid plaster onto the
sand impression, making sure the plaster fills
all of the indented areas. Let the plaster
dry undisturbed overnight. Lift the dried
sandcast out of the box and gently brush
away any excess sand.

9

Totem Pole Coatrack
American Indian Day is September 26.

Supplies: 2 lb., 10 oz. oatmeal canisters (six for each rack)
Black enamel spray paint
Triple laminated cardboard or regular cardboard
Dowel rods (a 5-foot length for each rack)
Sand (for weight)
Colored paper, Con-Tact paper, fabric scraps
Scissors, glue
Handsaw or sabre saw
   for the tri-wall

You'll need to glue a circle of cardboard between these two oatmeal canisters.

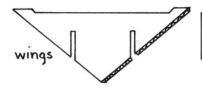

wings

beak

for stability, put some sand or gravel in the bottom two canisters

two layers of tri-wall glued together

Procedure: Spray paint the oatmeal canisters beforehand. Have each student complete a section of the totem pole. (Have on hand a couple of books on the Northwest Coast Indians for sample totem pole designs.) Cut two 12-inch circles from triple-laminated cardboard for the base. (Glue several layers of regular cardboard together if you don't have tri-wall.) Drill or gouge a hole in the center of the base large enough to hold a dowel rod and insert the rod into this hole. Gouge holes in the center of each oatmeal canister (top and bottom) and begin sliding them onto the dowel rod, one at a time. Make the wings and beak and assemble as shown in sketch.

Primitive Sculpture

Supplies: Clean, dry milk cartons or jugs with the tops
cut off (These will serve as molds.)
Plaster of Paris
Vermiculite (You can get this at a lumber
company.)
Carving tools
Sandpaper
Watercolors

Procedure: Show slides or have pictures on hand of
American Indian sculpture and design. This
will provide an awareness and appreciation
of the simplicity and sophistication that can
be achieved in sculpture. To make the carving
material, mix equal parts of plaster of Paris
and vermiculite. Add water until the mixture
is the consistency of buttermilk. Pour it into
your milk carton mold and let dry for 24 hours.
When dry, peel off the paper carton and carve
into a simple, primitive sculpture. Rough
edges can be smoothed with sandpaper
and designs can be added with watercolors and a small brush.

Matted Nature Picture
How to make the picture ...

Supplies: Cardboard (9"x 12" piece for each student)
Leaves, weeds, small flowers, grasses
Newspaper, scissors, glue
Light colored fabric (for a background)
Masking tape

light fabric background 8"x 11"

cardboard 9" x 12"

Procedure: Collect the flowers, weeds and grasses and
dry them out by laying them flat between newspapers and leaving them this way for one week.
Place books or other heavy objects on top of the
newspapers to make sure the leaves get flattened
out. Cut cardboard 9 inches by 12 inches for the
picture. Glue an 8" x 11" piece of light colored
fabric onto the center of the cardboard. Now
take the dried and pressed nature objects
and arrange them on the fabric until you
come up with an arrangement that pleases
you. (Keep in mind that after your picture is
matted your image area will be only 5 inches
by 8 inches.) Glue the objects down gently by
placing small dots of glue on the backs of the
leaves and pressing them gently to the fabric.

Matted Nature Picture
How to make the mat ...

Supplies: Cardboard (a 9" x 12" piece for each student)
Masking tape, glue
Fabric pieces (about 11" x 14" for each student);
    ginghams and calicos will work best
Scissors
Mat knife, utility knife or box cutter
Heavy-duty plastic wrap or lightweight
    acetate

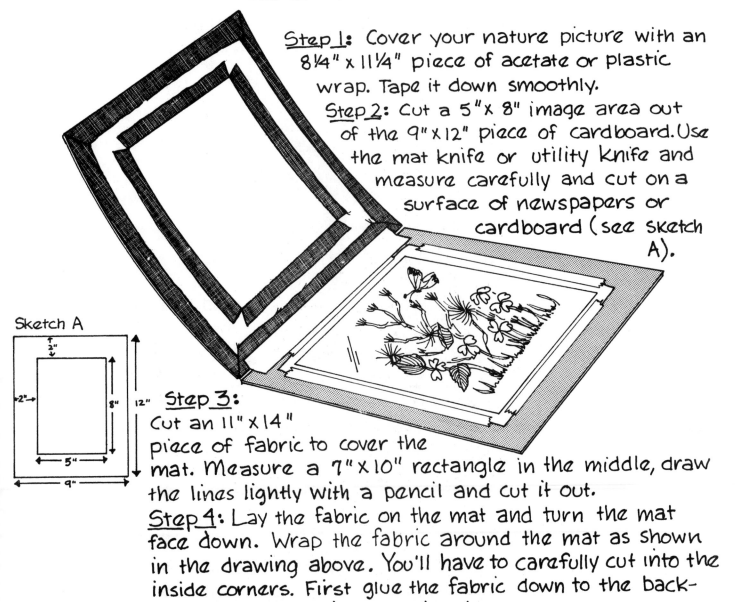

Step 1: Cover your nature picture with an 8¼" x 11¼" piece of acetate or plastic wrap. Tape it down smoothly.

Step 2: Cut a 5" x 8" image area out of the 9" x 12" piece of cardboard. Use the mat knife or utility knife and measure carefully and cut on a surface of newspapers or cardboard (see sketch A).

Sketch A

Step 3: Cut an 11" x 14" piece of fabric to cover the mat. Measure a 7" x 10" rectangle in the middle, draw the lines lightly with a pencil and cut it out.

Step 4: Lay the fabric on the mat and turn the mat face down. Wrap the fabric around the mat as shown in the drawing above. You'll have to carefully cut into the inside corners. First glue the fabric down to the backside, then tape with masking tape.

Step 5: Tape the two pieces of cardboard together as shown above.

September Bulletin Board Idea

Supplies: Light blue background paper
White paper for clouds
Brown butcher or construction paper
Lots of fall leaves
Pins, tacks or white glue

Procedure: Bring the beautiful colors of fall into your
classroom with this no-effort bulletin board.
Use the drawing of the tree trunk above;
put it on your opaque projector and reproduce it to fit your bulletin board. Tape several pieces of brown construction paper together on the back for the trunk. Make the clouds
from white butcher paper. Have the students
bring in lots of brightly colored fall leaves.
Either glue or pin the leaves on the tree.
The thicker the leaves, the better the effect.

"I'm done already!" Cards

Productive time-fillers for those who finish first.

Styrofoam Meat Tray Prints

You'll need a clean, dry styrofoam meat tray for this. (Your teacher can get these from the grocery store butcher for free.) Draw a design on the backside of the meat tray. Bear down hard with your pencil; you must make deep grooves in the styrofoam. With a brayer, cover the backside of the meat tray with printing ink. Turn it over and print on a piece of paper.

Fall Colors on Wet Paper

Take a piece of sturdy paper and wet it underwater. Wipe the excess water off into the sink. Now take watercolors, a brush and several thicknesses of newspaper and go to a flat surface. Drop autumn colors onto the wet paper and watch them blend and move together. Fill most of the page this way. Let the painting dry and then draw tree trunks and limbs onto the colors.

Leaf Print Notepaper

Take a piece of light colored paper (manilla, newsprint or typing paper) and make a print of a single leaf in the lower right-hand corner. Fold the paper in half so the leaf appears on the front. Now write a letter to your very best friend or a pen pal!

Milk Jug Birdhouse

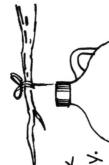

For this project you will need an empty gallon milk jug. Clean it out thoroughly. Cut a hole in the jug near the bottom large enough for a bird to fit through. Poke another hole beneath it; stick a twig in the hole, and hang.

"I'm done already!" Cards

Productive time-fillers for those who finish first.

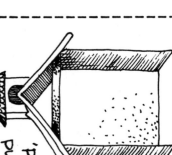

September

Preserved Leaves

Place leaves between two layers of waxed paper. Now put this in between several layers of newspaper. Iron this at medium heat. This will flatten the leaves and melt the two pieces of waxed paper together. Make a mat from construction paper or cardboard.

Paper Fans

←staple

The weather can still get pretty hot in September, so make a fan to cool yourself. Fold a piece of paper accordion style and color a brilliant design on it. Staple it together about an inch and a half from the bottom and unfold.

September   Indian Finger Puppet

Draw a shape like the one at the bottom of the card. Using markers, pencils and watercolors, paint an Indian's face on the paper. Cut it out. Wrap it around your finger and tape it so it fits. Make several, one for each finger!

September   Schoolhouse Diorama

Find a small cardboard box and change it into an old-fashioned, one-room schoolhouse. Make a roof and cupola out of paper. Make little desks, a blackboard, teacher, and pupils and glue them into your schoolhouse.

October

Arts & Crafts
Halloween Pop-up

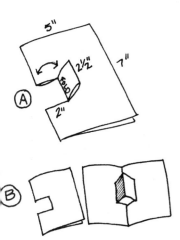

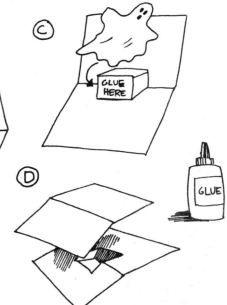

Supplies: Heavy paper
Scissors, glue, rulers
Crayons, markers or paint

Procedure: Fold 2 pieces of paper, 10" x 7" in half. Cut a square as shown in illustration Ⓐ in <u>one</u> of the sheets of paper. Fold the cut strip forward <u>and</u> backward, creasing it firmly each time. Open the card and push the strip to the inside. Close the card and crease firmly. (See illustration Ⓑ.) Decorate the inside of the card in a Halloween theme and color it in. Draw your ghost, goblin, bat, witch or whatever and glue it to your card as shown in illustration Ⓒ. Now glue both pieces of paper together as shown in illustration Ⓓ. Decorate the outside of the card.

TEACHER~ This is just one simple version of a pop-up card. There is a fun book devoted just to making pop-ups called <u>How to Make Pop-Ups</u> by Joan Irvine published by Morrow Junior Books. It is full of clever ideas that you and your students would really enjoy!

Hedge Apple Flowers

Supplies: Hedge apples (about 12 for a class of 30)
A sharp, serrated knife
Wire
Green florist's tape
Green and red construction paper
Old buttons
Clear acrylic spray
An oven, some old screen wire
Scissors, glue

NOTE: Hedge apples are
<u>not</u> edible. Teacher,
wash your hands thoroughly
after slicing them.

leaves

Procedure: Slice the hedge apples as thinly as possible.
A serrated knife will help. Poke a hole in the
center of each slice. Place them on screen
wire and bake them at 200° for one hour.
Stick a nine to ten-inch wire in the center
of a slice and make the leaves as shown.
Push the leaves up the wire to directly under
the hedge apple slice and wrap the wire
in green florist's tape. Cut an irregular
star shape from red construction paper and
glue it to the center of the slice. Now
glue a button to the top of the construction
paper star. Spray with clear acrylic spray.

Plaster Scrimshaw

The second Monday in October is Columbus Day.

Supplies: Plaster of Paris, water
Wax paper
Spoon
Carving tool (compass point, nail, nail file)
Paint, string, small paintbrushes

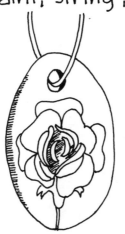

Procedure: During long sea voyages sailors alleviated their boredom by carving small, intricate pictures into sharks' teeth or whale bone. To make your own simple scrimshaw, mix one cup of plaster of Paris with ⅔ cup of water. Quickly stir the mixture until it's smooth and creamy and drop it by teaspoonfuls onto wax paper. While it's hardening poke a hole in the top for a string. Let the plaster harden for fifteen minutes. Then use a carving tool to etch a detailed design into the pendant. When the design is finished the paint can be applied. With a small brush, apply the paint to the lines that have been etched into the plaster. Then paint the other areas of the pendant, leaving some white space.

Bookmarkers
National Children's Book Week is the last week in October.

Supplies: Popsicle sticks
Poster board
White glue, scissors
Watercolors, markers

Procedure: Think of a simple design, object or creature that would make a nice bookmark. Draw it carefully on poster board and color it with paints and markers. Cut it out. Use white glue and glue the bookmark to the Popsicle stick. Place a book or heavy object on top until the glue dries.

Note to the Teacher: If you happen to have clear Con-Tact paper available, the bookmarks will last longer if you can cover the design with a layer and burnish it down well.

Apple Head Witches

Supplies:
Apples (one for each student)
Black-eyed peas
Rice
Fake fur scraps for hair
Black construction paper
Black fabric (enough for about 1 square foot per student)
Clear acrylic spray
Popsicle sticks (If you can't get ahold of these, any sticks will do.)
Scissors, glue, clear tape or black tape

How to cut the slits

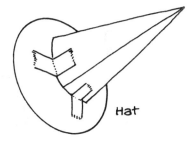

Hat

Procedure:

Peel a large apple, but leave the stem on. This will make it easy to hang the apple up to dry. After peeling the apple, cut slits in it as shown in the sketch. These can be cut with scissors, compass points, or dull knives. Let it dry for 24 hours. Then shape the face with your fingers. Push black-eyed peas in the slits for eyes, rice in the slit for the mouth. Now hang it from the stem for two weeks. Spray with clear acrylic spray. Glue fake fur scraps on for hair. Make the witch's hat from a black construction paper circle and cone as shown. Push the head onto a stick. Cut a small slit in the black fabric and tape it to the "neck" with black or clear tape.

Jumpin' Goblins

Supplies: Poster board or bristol board
Scissors, hole punch
Markers, paints or crayons
Grommets, string

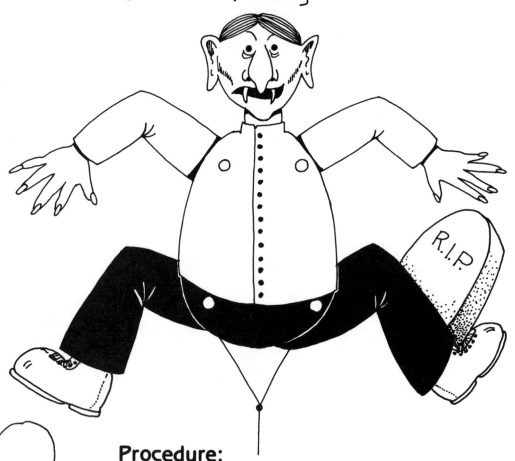

back view

Note to the Teacher:

Procedure:

Use the drawing above to help you make your pattern. Draw the five pieces for your goblin on the cardboard or Bristol board. Outline them with black marker and color them with paint, crayons or markers. Cut the pieces out. Punch four holes like the ones shown in the drawing above and push the grommets through the front. Poke a smaller hole under each grommet and push string through it as shown in back view. Connect string as shown and pull gently. Encourage the students to be creative and create their own "goblins." Once they understand the concept it will be easy.

22

Margarine Tub Creatures

Supplies: Margarine tubs (one for each student)
Construction paper, poster board
Paint, markers
Scissors, glue

Procedure: With a little imagination one margarine tub can become a menagerie of creatures! Just cut the head, arms, wings or whatever out of construction paper and add the details with markers or paint. Arrange them on the margarine tub lid as shown in the sketch above. Snap the tub onto the lid and everything will stay in place. When not in use, all the parts can be stored inside the tub.

Paper Plate Masks

Supplies: Paper plates (The cheap ones will do, but the Chinet ones will work better.)
Construction paper
Yarn, string, pipe cleaners
Glue, scissors, tape
Markers, crayons

Procedure: 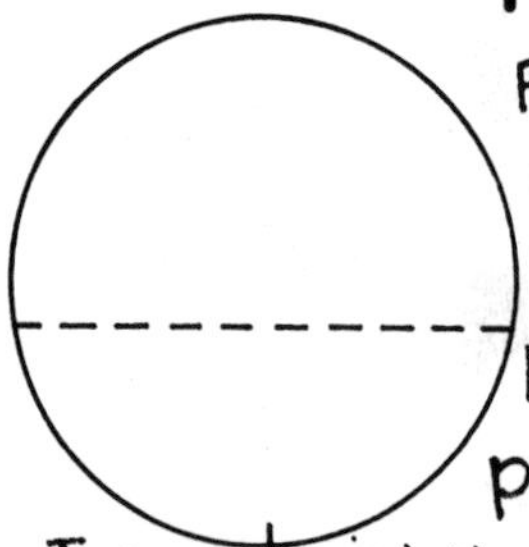
For the clown mask, cut a little less than half off of a paper plate. Tape brightly colored, heavy yarn pieces to the back for hair. Cut diamond-shaped holes for eyes and decorate the face with markers or crayons. Use a yarn pompon or a big red circle for a nose. Punch holes about halfway to the top for strings.

Procedure:

For the cat, again cut a paper plate the same size as for the clown mask. Cut two triangles for each ear and glue them to the back of the plate. Use colored construction paper to cut circles for the cheeks and triangles for the nose. Assemble and glue them together as shown; then glue them to the paper plate. Glue pipe cleaners onto the cheeks for whiskers. Cut circular holes for eyes and color the face.
Put the stripes and eyelashes on with marker or paint.

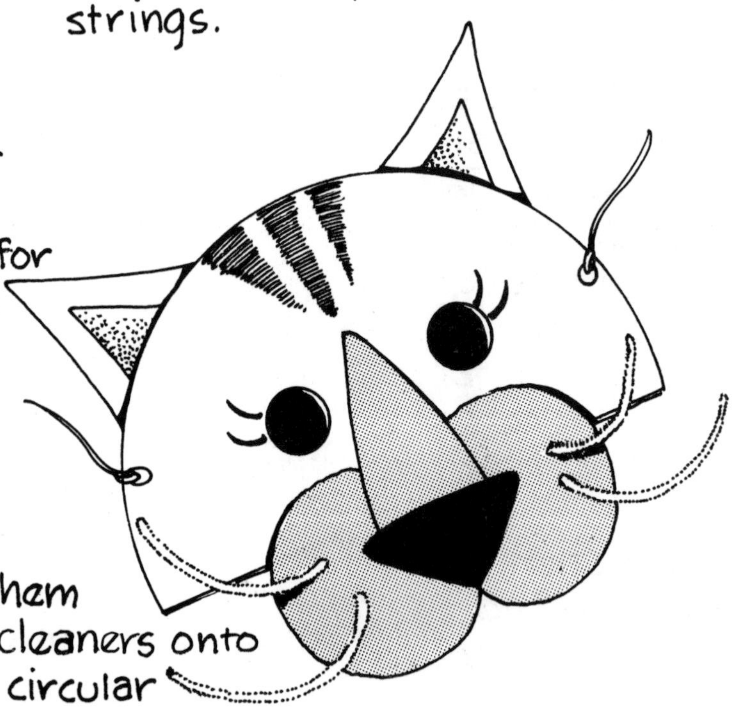

...more paper plate masks

Procedure:

Cut the paper plate as shown on the previous page. Cut the nose from poster board or another paper plate and glue it onto the plate. Make the ears from construction paper and glue them onto the back of the plate. Now draw on the sunglasses and color the face, nose and ears. Make the mustache from yarn taped to the back of the plate. The hat can be cut from construction paper and glued to the plate.

Procedure:

Cut the paper plate the same size that you cut the others. Make the ears, face and tongue from poster board or another paper plate. Tape the ears to the back of the plate and glue the face onto it. The tongue can be glued to the back of the face. Color or paint the eyes, face and ears. Make the spots and nose from dark colored construction paper and glue them on. The whiskers can be cut from construction paper.

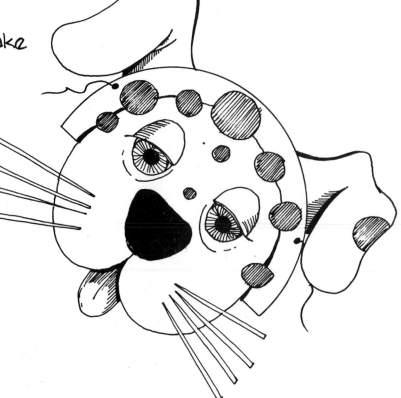

Haunted House Dioramas

Supplies: Cardboard boxes
Poster board, construction paper, oatmeal canisters
Old wallpaper sample books, fabric scraps,
   string, wood scraps, toothpicks, thread
Scissors, glue, paint

Procedure: This project can become as involved as you
wish to make it. It's a good idea to have a
couple of books on Victorian architecture on
hand as a guide. The exterior can be created
from cardboard boxes, canisters, and construction
paper. Furniture can be fashioned from paper,
wood scraps or cardboard and covered with
fabric scraps.

Note to the Teacher: Encourage the students to concentrate on
detail. Construction from a variety of "scraps"
can be a good lesson in resourcefulness
and elaboration.

Hoot Owl Catchalls

Supplies: 2 plastic bottles for each owl; half-gallon or gallon sized
Acrylic paint or tempera and shellac
Colored paper or fabric scraps
Scissors, glue, markers

wings

Procedure: For the hoot owl catchalls, cut the plastic bottles as shown above, removing handles and necks if they are present. For the heads, use a second plastic jug, the same size as the first. Cut ½ to 1 inch feathers along the bottom of the top half, and paint with acrylics or tempera paint with a top coat of shellac. Cut eyes, nose, and ears from construction paper and glue to container with white glue. (Ears are triangles curled around a pencil to give them their shape.) The wings are one piece of construction paper cut like a cape and glued around the owl. Feathers and claws on the front are painted on with acrylic or permanent marker.

Note to the Teacher: All kinds of animals can easily be made using this same idea. Lions, bears, ducks, roosters, all can be created using cut construction paper and a little imagination.

Bat Mobiles

Supplies:
Heavy string
Wax paper
White glue, scissors
Pencils
Paper
Tape
Black tempera paint or black dye

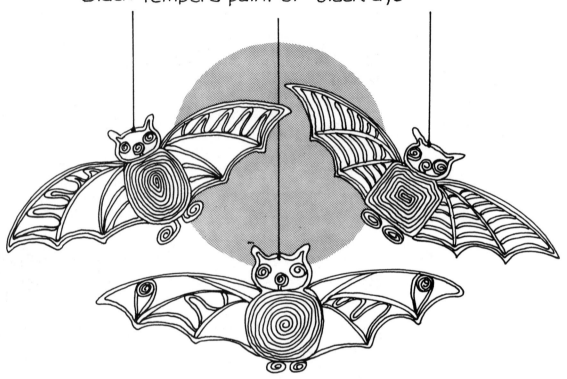

Procedure: Draw a sketch of a bat on a piece of paper (or any other Halloween character). Cover the drawing with a piece of wax paper and tape it in place. Dip string in glue and follow the lines of your sketch, laying the string on the wax paper. Lay the drawing flat, and let it dry at least overnight. When the glue is dry, carefully peel the bat off of the wax paper. Hang several bats at varying lengths from a dowel rod or coat hanger.

Note to the Teacher: If you want to color the bats black, either dye the string before or paint them black when they're dry.

October Crayon Etching

Supplies: Crayons
Drawing paper
Something to scrape with (scissors, compass point, nail file, etc.)

Procedure: Using light or bright colored crayons, cover the entire piece of paper, coloring heavily. This layer of crayons should be thick. Now cover this with black or dark colored crayon until the paper is completely covered. Burnishing the bottom layer with a paper towel will help the top layer of crayon adhere. Next, scratch a design onto the paper, using a sharp tool.

Note to the Teacher: Tell the students to have a definite fall or Halloween scene or design in mind before beginning to scratch away at the dark layer of crayon.

October Bulletin Board Idea

Supplies: Black or dark blue background paper
Brown, gray, dark green, and yellow construction paper
Scissors, pins or tacks

Procedure: Combine Children's Book Week and Halloween with this grisly but fun bulletin board idea. Use dark blue or black corrugated paper for a background. Make a simple tree from brown kraft or construction paper. Staple on dark green construction paper for a foreground. The students can cut their own tombstones from gray construction paper. They should cut one tombstone for each book they read during October. The epitaph should describe the book in some way, and the book title should be printed at the bottom of the tombstone.

"I'm done already!" Cards

Productive time-fillers for those who finish first.

October

Leaf Pictures

Collect some leaves from outdoors. Glue them down to a piece of construction paper so they make a picture. Now color in a background.

October

Fall Wall Decoration for Mom

Bunch together dried grasses, weeds, wheat, barley, etc., around a long wooden spoon. Tape them, a few at a time, to the spoon handle. Tie a nice ribbon in a big bow to cover the tape. To hang it up, loop a string around the handle.

Dried Weed Collage

Cover a long, rectangular piece of poster board or cardboard with brown burlap. Glue dried weeds and flowers (using white glue) to the burlap in an attractive arrangement.

October

Upside Downers

Turn this card upside down to see what becomes of these characters. Now try drawing several of your own upside downers.

"I'm done already!" Cards

Productive time-fillers for those who finish first.

October

New World Sketch Diary

Columbus Day is celebrated on the second Monday in October. Use your imagination and try to visualize some of the first things Columbus would have seen when he discovered the new world. Sketch these scenes on a piece of paper and then paint them with watercolors.

October

Trick or Treat!

Find a plain, brown grocery bag and decorate it for your trick or treat bag for Halloween night. Use color crayons, permanent markers and colored construction paper to make your trick or treat bag special!

October

Fire Prevention Poster

The week of October 9 is Fire Prevention Week. Putting to use the fire safety rules you know, make a fire prevention poster to hang up in your classroom.

October

Jack-O'-Lantern Mobile

Cut pumpkin shapes out of orange construction paper. Color the stems green. Cut the facial features out of black construction paper and glue them on. Hang them from strings, then hang the strings from a coat hanger.

November

Arts & Crafts

Autumn Wall Hanging

START
WITH THIS
PART OF
THE EGG
CARTON.

Supplies: Egg cartons
Ribbon
Scissors, tape, string
A wide assortment of
   dried weeds

Procedure: A few days before this project
is planned, take a nature walk with your students to gather the
weeds and grasses. Cutout the part of the egg carton shown above and
paint it with acrylic or tempera paint. Give it plenty of time to dry.
Staple or glue the bow to the lower part of the lid. Start at the top,
putting the longest stems into the top or second hole. Work your
way down adding a little glue to the lip of each opening to hold the
weeds in place. These make lovely Thanksgiving decorations.

Seed Necklace

Supplies: All kinds of seeds and pods (pumpkin, sunflower, allspice, cantaloupe, coffee beans, acorn squash, apple, watermelon, acorn cups, etc.)
Needles
Heavy carpet thread

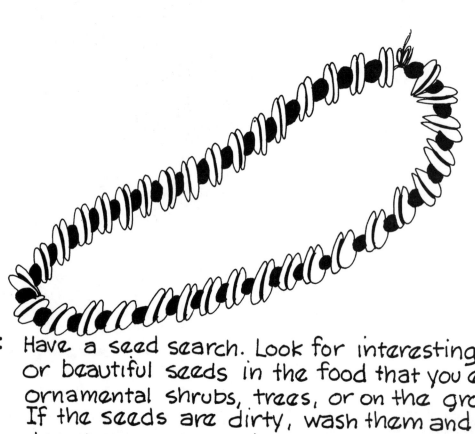

Procedure: Have a seed search. Look for interesting or beautiful seeds in the food that you eat, ornamental shrubs, trees, or on the ground. If the seeds are dirty, wash them and dry them on paper towels. Separate the seeds into groups of their kind and think about an interesting pattern to string them in. Some of the seeds may be too hard to push a needle through. In that case, soak them for several hours in warm water before trying to string them. Then thread a sturdy needle with carpet thread and carefully string the seeds into a pattern of your liking; tie.

Cardboard Loom Weaving

Supplies: Strong cardboard pieces, 7x10 inches
Scissors, utility knife
Cotton twine
Colored yarn

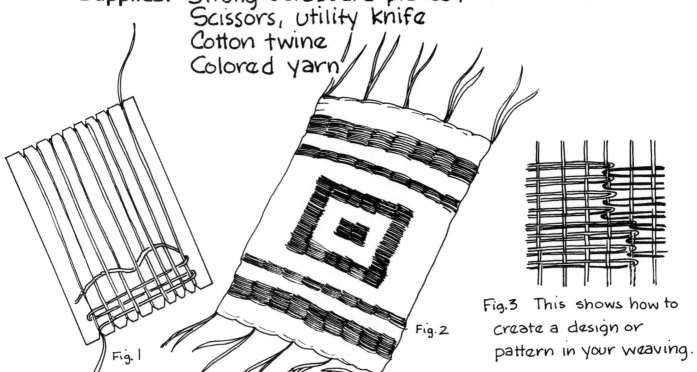

Fig. 1

Fig. 2

Fig.3 This shows how to create a design or pattern in your weaving.

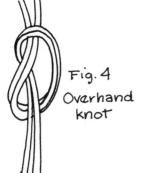

Fig. 4
Overhand knot

Procedure: Cut notches ½ inch apart and ¼ inch deep at the top and bottom edges of the cardboard. Wind cotton twine around the loom starting at the bottom left, leaving a tail 10 inches long. Completely wind the loom, leaving a 10-inch tail in the upper right-hand corner. Pull the 2 tails to the back and knot them together. Then begin weaving the yarn over and under. At the end of the row the yarn circles the last thread and comes back. Push the woven rows of yarn down to compact them. To prevent the weaving from pulling in at the middle, weave a "hill" into the weft as shown in fig 1. Never tie the yarn when changing colors, the weaving should be packed down tightly enough to hold it together. When it is completed, the ends are cut flush to the weaving. Then turn the loom over and cut the string in the middle of the loom. Turn the loom back over, and starting at the left bottom, tie two strings at a time in an overhand knot, as shown in fig. 4.

Corn Shuck Dolls

Supplies:
Corn shucks
Pipe cleaners
Small styrofoam balls for heads
Corn silks
Thread
Glycerine
Scissors , glue

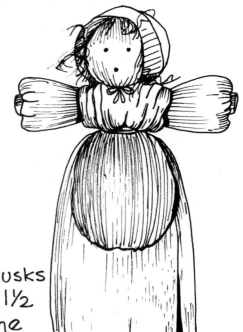

Procedure: Soak dry corn husks in a solution of 1½ teaspoons glycerine to one quart warm water to make them pliable. The husks can be dyed by soaking them in water tinted with food coloring. Lay the husks on newspapers and blot the excess moisture out of them with paper toweling. Keep the husks in plastic bags because they must remain moist while they're being sculpted.

FOR THE HEAD: Cut a 4-inch piece of pipe cleaner and push it halfway into a ¾-inch styrofoam ball to make the head and torso armature. Cover the styrofoam ball with two pieces of husk, each 5 inches long by 1½ inches wide. Tie the husk at the neck first, then at the top of the head as shown in the picture to the left. Bring the strips of husk back down "inside out"

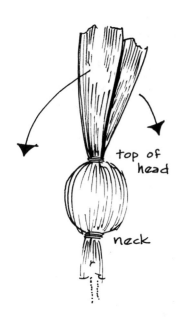

top of
head

neck

from the top and wrap with a thread at the neck; tie.

FOR THE ARMS: Cut a 4-inch length of pipe cleaner for the arms. Roll it up in a 1-inch by 4-inch piece of corn husk and tie with thread ½ inch from each end to make wrists.

FOR THE SLEEVES: For each sleeve cut two pieces of husk 2x3 inches each. Gather and overlap them just above the wrists as shown below. Wrap the ends tightly with

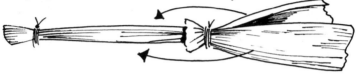

several layers of thread and tie. Bring the ends of the husks back "inside out" and tie tightly to the center of the arm piece. Lay the arms across the body beneath the wrapped head. Attach it to the body securely by crisscrossing thread around it several times and tie tightly.

TORSO: Lay the body and arms between two pieces of husk 1½ x 2 inches each. Arrange the pieces so the husk extends 2 inches above the head. Wrap the thread tightly around these husks at the neck. Bring the husks down, pad with a little cotton and tie at the waist.

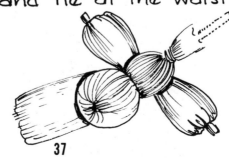

... corn shuck dolls (cont'd.)

SKIRT: Bend the arms up toward the head. Now overlap 6 or 7 corn husks around the doll's waist, making sure the wider ends are above the doll's head and arms.

Wrap at the waist as tightly as possible with about 10 turns of thread; tie. Bring the husks down one at a time to form a full skirt. For an apron, use a piece cut like the one shown below. The strips that you've cut form the

cut here

apron strings. Tear another narrow piece of husk to tie around the doll's waist. This will camouflage the raw edge of the apron. Bring the arms down to the desired position. Trim the skirt evenly at the bottom so the doll stands 5 to 6 inches tall. If the skirt flares too much, wrap a piece of husk around the bottom until the doll dries. The doll should stand alone.

HAIR: With white glue adhere some corn silks to the top of the doll's head.

FEATURES: Either poke holes for eyes and mouth or paint dots of India ink.

BONNET: Cut a piece the shape of the sketch to the left. Wrap it around the head as shown and tie with a strip of corn husk.

BONNET

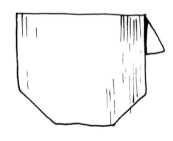

Pine Cone Turkey

Supplies: Pine cones (one per student)
Red felt
Needles and red thread
Sequins
Colored construction paper
Scissors, glue

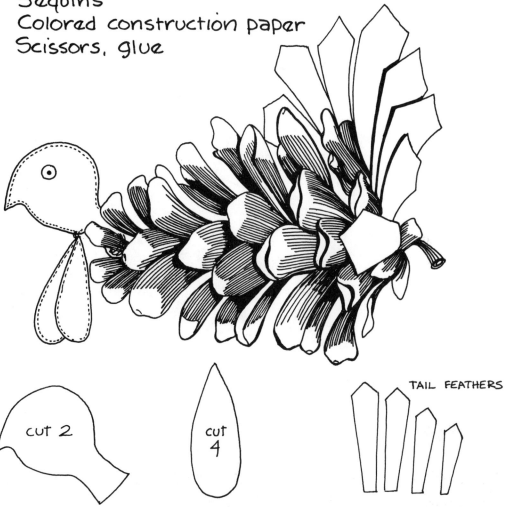

cut 2

cut 4

TAIL FEATHERS

Procedure: Cut 2 heads and 4 wattles from red felt. With needle and red thread, sew the two heads together, then make the two wattles in the same way. Sew the wattles to the head as shown. Glue sequins to both sides of the turkey's head for eyes. Stitch the neck of the turkey to one or two of the petals to hold it in place. Make the tail feathers in graduating lengths as shown above and glue them onto the pine cone petals with white glue.

Wooden Shingle Painting

Supplies: Old barn siding or barn shingles (If this is unavailable any weathered wood scraps will do.)
Drill
Heavy twine, clear acrylic spray
Acrylic paint, brushes, water
Dried weeds or flowers

Procedure: On an old piece of wood, sketch and then paint a harvest or Thanksgiving scene. Dried weeds or flowers, stones, beans, or other objects may be added to the composition if desired. A protective coat of clear acrylic spray should be used to protect the painting. Drill two holes in the top of the shingle as shown and lace a piece of heavy twine through the holes and knot the ends.

Indian Quill Designs

Supplies: Flat toothpicks , glue
Food coloring
Leather scraps (very inexpensive from
    leather craft stores)

Procedure: Porcupine quill decoration was an art known
to North American Indians. The quills were
dyed and sewn to leather or birch bark in
elaborate designs. Dyed, flat toothpicks can
give a similar effect for a modern day project.
Soak the toothpicks in food coloring and dry
them on newspaper. In the meantime cut
the leather scraps into small pendant shapes,
wristbands or headbands. Plan out a design
and break or cut the toothpicks to the right
length; glue them down as desired. Re-
member to glue them in the opposite direction of how the leather will curve or the
toothpicks will break.

Note to the Teacher: Provide pictures of porcupine quill decoration to help the students understand
and appreciate this project.

Decorated Gourds

Supplies: Gourds (one for each student)
Wood stain, the color of your choice
One wood block for each student (for a base)
One dowel for each student
Clear plastic spray or shellac
Paint and paintbrushes
A drill to drill the hole in the base
White glue, sharp pencils or compass points

Procedure: Dry gourds for several weeks in a warm, dry place, turning them to avoid mildew. Once they're dry submerge them in water for one hour. Rub off the outer skin with a pot cleaner; let dry. With a pencil, draw your design on the gourd. Choose the areas of your design you wish to darken or paint and stain or paint them. When the stain or paint is completely dry, use a sharp pencil or compass point to gouge out all the outlines. These cuts will reveal the inner, lighter part of the gourd. To make the stand, drill holes large enough for the dowel in the gourd and the wood block. Put glue on one end of the gourd and insert it into the wood block first. Stain both and let dry. Now put glue on the other end and insert into gourd. Apply two coats of shellac or clear plastic spray to finished gourd.

Marbelized Paper

Supplies: Powdered or oil paint
Large shallow pan (A photographer's tray
would work best.)
Paper
Small containers or jars for mixing
Turpentine
Soap or detergent
Comb, Afro pick, or toothpicks

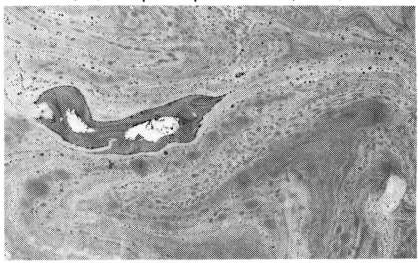

Procedure: Pour a little turpentine into a mixing jar
and add paint until the pigment is the
desired strength. Put about an inch of
water in the shallow tray. Drizzle the
colored turpentine onto the surface of the
water in some kind of pattern. (Experiment
with random and planned patterns.)
Stir the surface of the water with the
Afro pick, creating a spontaneous pattern.
Now lay the paper on, or drag the
paper across the surface of the water.
If multicolored designs are desired,
more than one color can be added to
the tray or the paper can be dipped
several times into single colors. This is
a project that will be a lot of fun to
experiment with. Clean up the containers
with detergent and hot water.

The Mayflower

Supplies: Paper plates
Crayons or tempera paints
Toothpicks and drinking straws
Plain or construction paper
Scissors, glue

Procedure: Make several patterns for the ship and sails (see A and B). Place the boat pattern on an inverted paper plate and cut two (see C). Color and decorate the ship as desired. Make cuts in the bottom, overlap the pieces and glue together (see D). Now glue the matching ends of the ship together. Cut the sails from white or colored paper. Glue toothpicks to the sails. Now glue the sails to the drinking straws. Place the "masts" inside the boat and glue or staple in place.

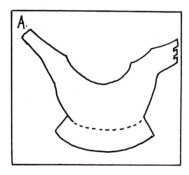

A.

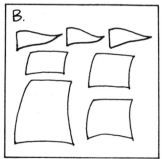

B.

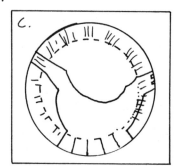

C.

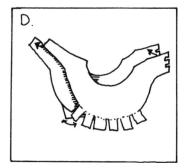

D.

Tiny Pilgrims

Supplies: Construction paper
Small styrofoam balls
Yarn scraps
Scissors, glue

Procedure: Make cones from construction paper circles for the bodies, using Scotch tape to fasten (see A).
Poke a hole, ½ inch deep, in the styrofoam ball with a pencil. Glue to top of cone. Make arms as shown below (B) and Scotch tape to the back of the cone. The Pilgrim's hat can be made from a construction paper cone or a 1 oz. paper cup (see C). Glue the hat to the yarn layer. Make capes from construction paper or fabric scraps. Hair can be added with yarn and facial features created with construction paper.

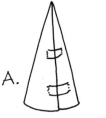

A.

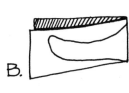

B.

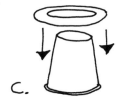

C.

November Bulletin Board Idea

Supplies: Background paper (any color)
Construction paper (all colors)
Scissors, tacks or pins

Procedure: Using the drawing above as an example, draw a big cornucopia to tack up on your bulletin board. Make up patterns of fruits -- apples, oranges, limes, lemons, bananas. Have each student fill out one or more of these, each one representing something that child feels thankful for. Fill the board with these tokens of thankfulness.

"I'm done already!" Cards

Productive time-fillers for those who finish first.

November

Doorknob Vase

Spray paint an old doorknob and arrange some silk or dried flowers in it.

November

Walnut Shell Mouse

Paint eyes and glue whiskers on half of a walnut shell. Add a gray felt tail. Glue a red bead on for a nose. Make ears from gray construction paper.

November

Jewelry Box

Paint a cigar box any color. Glue sequins, old jewelry, buttons, etc., on the top and sides. Line the inside with felt or velvet.

November

Patchwork Flower Pots

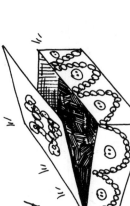

Cut scraps of fabric into interesting shapes. Glue them down into place with white glue. When dry, give the pot a coat of shellac or polymer medium.

"I'm done already!" Cards

Productive time-fillers for those who finish first.

November

Seashell Turtle

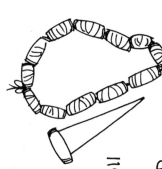

Use a seashell and make a pattern from cardboard. Cut it out and glue the shell to the pattern base. Glue a pencil eraser on for a head and pipe cleaners for feet and a tail. Press map pins in the eraser for eyes.

November

Egg Carton Jewelry

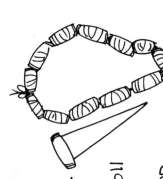

With a paper punch, punch out lots of little circles from a colored Styrofoam egg carton. With a sharp needle and thread, string them alone or alternately with other beads; tie.

November

Letter or Recipe Card Holder for Mom

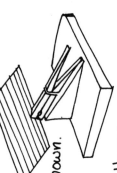

Find a scrap of wood for a base and glue a triangle of wood to the top of it as shown. Glue a clothespin to the triangle. Sand them all down smooth and paint or stain them.

November

Paper Necklace

Cut 4-inch long triangular-shaped pieces from colored magazine pages. Roll them up and glue. When you have plenty rolled up, put them on a string and tie.

48

December

Arts & Crafts
Pine Cone Christmas Tree

Supplies: Small boxes
Pine cones
Glue, scissors
Colored paper or fabric to line boxes with
Little wood scraps to wrap and put under "tree"
Rickrack, colored paper, beads, sequins or bittersweet berries

Procedure: Line a small, shallow box with fabric or colored paper. Glue a pine cone to the inside of the shadow box. Decorate the pine cone "tree" by glueing on beads, sequins, bittersweet berries, rickrack or metallic cord. Cut a star to glue at the top of the "tree." Wrap 2 or 3 wood scraps with Christmas wrapping and glue them to the bottom of the shadow box at the base of the tree. Glue a cord to the back of the shadow box for hanging.

Frosty Jumping Jack

Supplies: Poster board or bristol board
Scissors, hole punch
Markers, paints or crayons
Grommets, string

back view

Procedure: Using the drawing above to make your pattern, cut out the five pieces needed for your jumping jack. Draw in the details with black marker and color the snowman with paints, crayon, or markers. Punch four holes as shown in the drawing above and push the grommets through the front. Poke a smaller hole under each grommet and push string through each as shown in back view. Connect string as shown and pull gently.

Giant Wall Star

Supplies: Butcher paper, colored or white
Construction paper
Hole punch
Key ring
Scotch tape or stapler
Scissors, glue

Procedure: Unroll a 25-foot length of butcher paper and cut it 18 inches wide. Double it over so it's 12½ feet long. Now start at one end and pleat it carefully. When this is done, punch a hole in one end through all of the layers and insert a key ring. Open the star and tape or staple the ends together. Glue something ornamental to the center (a star, Santa Claus, foil snowflake, etc.) and hang it up on the wall.

Note to the Teacher: This project can be varied in many ways; if you wish to make it smaller, decrease the width and length of the paper. You can also use the Paper Towel Dip 'n Dye (p.128) for a different effect. For another variation see the summer sunburst (p.127).

Santa and Rudolph

Supplies: Clothespins
A saw (It would probably be easier to do all the sawing beforehand with a power saw.)
White glue, epoxy glue
Cardboard, colored paper, wrapping paper scraps
Acrylic paints or tempera and shellac
Pipe cleaners

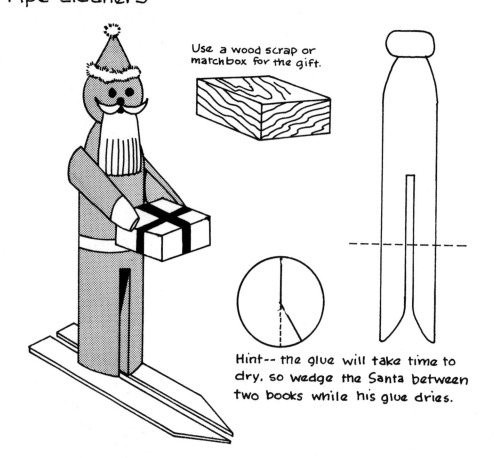

Use a wood scrap or matchbox for the gift.

Hint-- the glue will take time to dry, so wedge the Santa between two books while his glue dries.

Procedure: For the Santa, cut off the bottom of a clothespin as shown and glue the sawed off pieces on as arms. Make the skis with pieces of cardboard and glue them on the legs. Paint the clothespin red except for the hands and belt. Paint the eyes and nose with black paint. Make the mustache and beard from stiff, white paper. Wrap a matchbox for a gift and glue it in Santa's arms. The hat is made by forming a cone from a paper circle (see sketch above for how to cut, leaving overlap for glue).

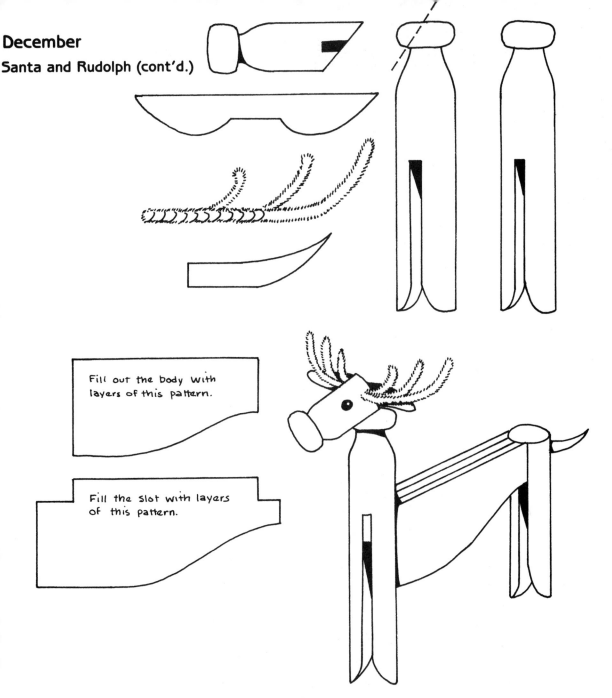

Fill out the body with layers of this pattern.

Fill the slot with layers of this pattern.

Procedure: The reindeer is made from three clothespins: one whole one, one cut off at the top to make the back legs, and a third cut at a slant for the head. Use three pipe cleaners of graduating lengths for the antlers; twist them together as shown and glue them into the slot in the head. Make the ears of heavy paper and glue them on, covering the slot. You'll need epoxy glue to secure the head to the other clothespin. The body is made of cardboard, several layers built up to fill the slot, then more layers to fatten up the sides. The tail is made of paper.

Ornaments

Supplies: Paper (A wallpaper book would provide great paper for this.)
Scissors, glue
String, stapler

Christmas Ball

Out of the paper of your choice, cut 9 circles 5 inches in diameter. Fold each one in half and crease it through the middle. Open them up, stack them on top of each other, and staple them on the crease in 3 places: top, middle, and bottom. Alternating top and bottom, glue the pieces together to about ⅓ of the way to the center. Hang from a thread run through the top of the ornament.

Swedish Christmas Bird

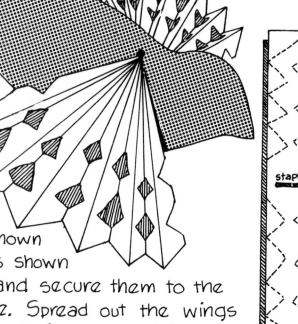

Enlarge the pattern above and use it for the body of the bird. Use bristol board or cardboard. Make the wings and tail of a thin paper, like tissue or typing paper. Cut 2 strips 5" wide by 9" long. Fold each strip in half, then in half again, until the strip is about ½" wide. Open up the strip and, using the creases as guides, refold in accordion pleats. Staple across the middle and cut out pieces as shown in sketch. Cut out slits in bird pattern as shown above. Slip the wings and tail through and secure them to the bird with small pieces of cellophane tape. Spread out the wings and fasten the center of the tail with tape to form a semicircle.

...more ornaments

Supplies: Paper, scissors
Stapler, thread

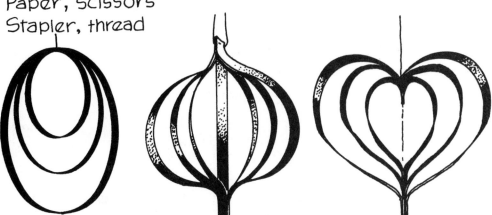

Procedure: The three ornaments above are all made from paper strips stapled together and hung from thread. For the three rings, cut 3 strips ¾" wide, in 3 lengths: 18", 15", and 12".

For the middle design, start with seven strips ¾" wide. The center strip is 5½" long, the next two are 6" long, and the outside strips are 7" long.

For the heart cut seven strips, each ½" wide. The outside strips are 9", the next two are 7½", the inside two are 6" and the center one is 4".

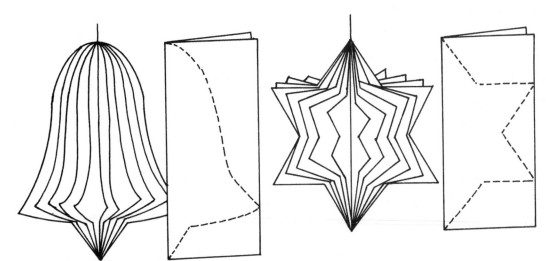

For the bell, start with 15 rectangles 4½" by 5"; cut 15 bells using the pattern above (enlarged). Fold each one in half, making a strong crease. Flatten them out, stack them up, and staple them 3 times along the crease. Open it up and hang. For the star start with 15 squares 4½" by 4½".

Santa Hideaway

Supplies: A large cardboard box
Colored and white paper
Two paper fasteners
Yarn scraps (optional)
Markers
Scissors, glue

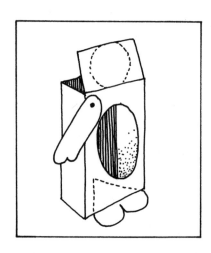

Procedure: Cut the front opening in a large cardboard box.
Use one of the top flaps for Santa's head (see
detail). Make hat from red and white paper.
Facial features, beard, and white cuffs can also be
cut from construction paper and glued onto the box.
Cover the front of the box with red paper and glue a
black belt on. Fashion the arms from cardboard, cover
with red paper, and attach to the box with fasteners.
Cut a heart shape from cardboard for feet.

56

Classroom Tree

Supplies: Chicken wire
Ornament hooks
Colored paper, gift wrap, aluminum foil
Scissors, stapler

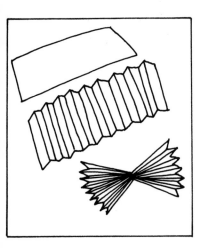

Procedure: This is a fun classroom project that will result in an impressive tree. Start with a five-foot chicken wire cone. Make five or ten-inch pleated stars as shown in detail. Cut paper for five-inch stars 5" x 12". Cut paper for ten-inch stars 10" x 20". Narrow pleats are more attractive. Fasten center with a bow or staple, open the star and fasten ends with a staple or tape. The stars can be attached to the chicken wire cone with ornament hooks or tape.

Special Wraps

Supplies: Boxes, pipe cleaners
Scissors, glue, tape
Wrapping paper, ribbon, yarn
Construction paper
Coffee can lids (for lion)

If you use rubber cement to glue paper to wings, the paper will adhere smoothly.

Make your holiday presents even more special with these super gift wrap ideas!

USE A PIPE CLEANER FOR A TAIL. TIE YARN SCRAPS TO THE END OF PIPE CLEANER.

TAPE YELLOW PAPER OVALS TO THE BOTTOM OF BOX FOR PAWS.

Procedure: ANGEL:
First wrap the box with wrapping paper. Cut wing shapes from cardboard and cover with more wrap. Cut an oval for the angel's face and draw the facial features with markers. Tape wings on back and use curling ribbon for hair.
LION: Wrap your gift with yellow paper. Cover a coffee can lid with a yellow paper circle and cut black construction paper for nose and eyes. Draw in the mouth. Tape brown yarn scraps to back of lid for a mane. Pin lid to box.

...more special wraps

Supplies: Boxes and coffee cans, cotton balls (optional)
Scissors, glue, tape
Wrapping paper, ribbon, yarn
Construction paper
Dowel rods or pencils for drumsticks

Procedure: <u>SANTA:</u> Gift wrap a box in red paper. Glue a strip of black construction paper one-third the way from the bottom for Santa's belt. Cut an oval from pink or tan construction paper for a face. Use white paper or cotton balls for beard and eyebrows. Eyes, nose, mustache and mouth can be cut from construction paper. Santa's hat is made from red and white paper.
<u>TOY DRUM:</u> Put your present inside the can and replace the lid. Wrap the sides in holiday wrap. Zigzag colored yarn around the can, taping at top and bottom. Cover the top and bottom with a strip of colored paper. Drumsticks are dowels or pencils with cut circles taped to end.

Patchwork Balls

Supplies:
Styrofoam balls
Ribbon
Fabric scraps
Florist's wire or some other thin wire
White glue, scissors

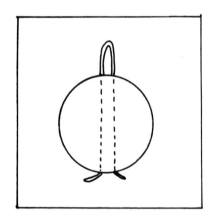

Procedure: Cut one-inch squares from various patterns of material scraps. Cut and bend the florist's wire in a length long enough to go completely through the styrofoam ball (see detail). Bend the bottom ends flush to the contour of the ball. Smear glue on the backsides of the fabric squares and adhere them to the ball, overlapping them slightly. Some of the squares can be cut with pinking shears if you have them. A final coat of Mod Podge or polymer medium is optional; this will give it a shiny coat. Tie a big, bright bow around the wire at the top of the ball. Easy!

Star Mobiles

Supplies: Drinking straws
Aluminum foil
¼" or less paper ribbon, silver or colored
Thread or thin string
Dowel rod, coat hanger, or kite stick
Scissors, glue

A.

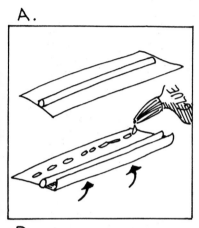

B.

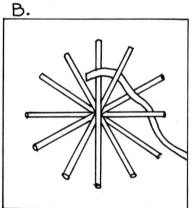

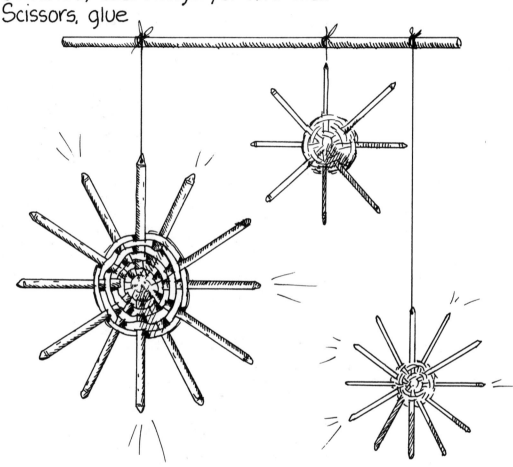

Procedure: For each star in the mobile, cover 6 straws with foil. (See A.) Cross the stars in the center and weave the ribbon in and out. (See B.) Glue or tape the ribbon end to secure it. Cut the foil tips to points and hang from thread. Make several stars and hang them from the hanger, dowel, or kite stick.

Note to the Teacher: The students' mobiles will be more attractive if you encourage them to vary the size of the stars; some smaller, some larger. If the amount of woven ribbon is varied, this, too, will add to the looks of the mobile.

December Bulletin Board Idea

Supplies: Scissors, tacks, glue or rubber cement
Red butcher paper or corrugated paper
Tinsel garland the width of your board
Construction paper
1 bag of cotton balls

Procedure: Cut a triangle from red paper to fit your bulletin board. Make the belt and boots with black construction paper, the buckles with yellow paper. Cut the simple hands and face from pink paper, and cut circles from black paper for the eyes, nose and mouth. Make a mustache from white paper and glue cotton balls on for a beard and pompon. Cut red circles for the rosy cheeks. Cut the banner from white butcher paper and tack a length of tinsel garland to the bottom of Santa's costume.

"I'm done already!" Cards

Productive time-fillers for those who finish first.

Potato Print Greeting Cards

For this project you'll need white linoleum block printing ink, black construction paper and a potato. Dig your design out of the potato and roll the white ink onto it. Stamp your design on the folded paper. Write your message on the inside with white chalk.

Stained Glass Designs

For this you'll need two sheets of black construction paper, glue, and colored art tissue. Make two identical designs from the black paper.(Cut one first and trace the next one.) Glue the colored tissue to the first one, then glue the second one to it, sandwich style.

Golden Eggs

Take an egg and poke a hole in both ends. Carefully blow the insides out onto a paper towel. Let it dry out for a day. Take a long needle and run a knotted thread up through the egg. Roll it in Elmer's glue and then gold glitter. Hang it to dry.

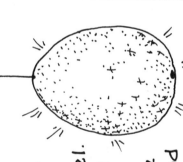

Patchwork Balls II

Cut fabric scraps into 3/4" squares. Lay the fabric squares on a styrofoam ball and push the edges of the squares into the ball with a seam ripper. Cover the entire ball this way.

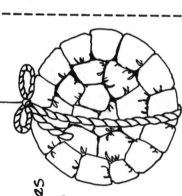

63

"I'm done already!" Cards

Productive time-fillers for those who finish first.

Winter Collage

December

Cut out figures and pictures from old Christmas cards or magazines. Make a winter collage with your cut outs on a piece of 18" x 24" poster board.

Cone Angel

December

Gold or silver wrapping paper works well for this. Make a cone from a circle cut as shown below. Cut the top off of the cone and glue on a little styrofoam ball or old Christmas tree ornament. Cut wings as shown and use a pipe cleaner for a halo.

Songbird

December

Using construction paper, cut out one body and two wings. Use the sketch here to help you draw your pattern. Staple or glue the wings to the body and bend them slightly outward. Suspend the bird from a thread.

Wise Men

December

Make these from colorful paper or foil. Start with a cone made from a circle (see Cone Angel). Cut the cape and crown as shown in sketches. Wrap them around the cone and glue them into place.

January

Arts & Crafts
Pebble Penguins

Supplies: Oblong-shaped rocks for penguins' bodies
Pebbles for feet and noses
Broken toothpicks for penguins' crests
Quick drying epoxy glue
Black, white and red acrylic paint
Gloss polymer medium

Procedure: Epoxy flat pebbles onto the larger oblong rocks for feet. Let dry. Lay a penguin on its back and epoxy a smaller pebble on for a nose. Let dry. Stand the penguin up and epoxy 2or3 broken toothpicks onto the top for a crest. Sketch in the areas to be painted black with a marker. Paint the white area of the penguin first, then the black. Add a red bow tie for color if you wish. Paint the eyes with a small brush or permanent marker. Let the paint dry completely and brush on a coat of gloss polymer medium.

Blizzard Designs

Supplies: String
Liquid tempera paint
Paper (colored or white)
A piece of heavy cardboard or wood

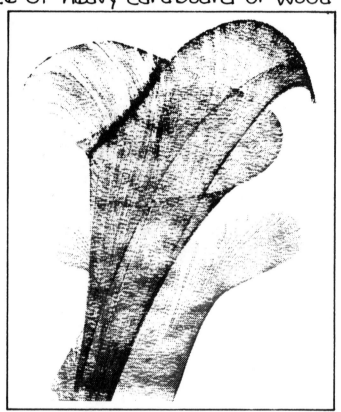

Procedure: These pulled string designs can create all kinds of effects: whirlwinds, blizzards, exotic flowers. Just experiment with the placement of the string and the colors that are used. Start by laying a piece of paper on a flat surface. Dip a length of string into the liquid tempera, leaving both ends uncoated. Arrange the soaked string on the piece of paper, with the two clean ends extending beyond the same edge of the paper. Put another piece of paper on top, sandwiching the string. Now cover these with a piece of sturdy cardboard or masonite and hold it in place firmly with one hand. With the other hand pull the two ends of the string from between the paper.

Winter Yarn Paintings

Supplies: Colored yarn
Corrugated cardboard
Scissors
White glue
Toothpicks

Fill areas from the outer edges in, not from the center out.

Procedure: Start with a fairly small piece of cardboard because of the amount of time involved in completing a yarn painting. Sketch a winter theme picture on the cardboard and decide what color yarn will appear in which areas. A border should be included in the design. It is important that every square inch of the yarn painting is filled with yarn. Paint one small area at a time with white glue and fill it in completely with yarn, keeping the top of the yarn soft and free of glue. Use the toothpicks to guide the yarn into place; this will keep the yarn from sticking to your fingers.

Snowflakes

Supplies: White paper, newspaper
Black paper
Scissors
Glue

Procedure: Before using the white paper to cut the actual snowflake designs, experiment by cutting some practice designs out of old newspapers. First, cut a circular piece of paper and fold it 3 or 4 times into a pie-shaped piece. Draw a design on the pie-shaped wedge first. Then cut away parts of the design until the snowflake takes on the desired shape. Cut several snowflakes of varying sizes and designs. Glue them onto a sheet of black construction paper in an interesting pattern.

Layered Paper Designs

Supplies: Colored paper
Scissors
Rubber cement
Pencil
Colored poster board (to mount the design on)

Procedure: The layers of the design must be cut one at a time, starting with the top layer of paper. For this reason, it would be a good idea to make a rough sketch of the design before beginning. After cutting the top layer of paper, paper clip the next layer to the underside of it. With a pencil, draw the contours of the cuts to be made on the next layer of paper; cut. Follow the same procedure for each layer of the design. Rubber cement the layers together and mount the entire design on a piece of colored poster board.

Note to the Teacher: This is a project that is easier to understand after having done one or two. A simple practice project should be cut first.

West African Adinkra Prints

January 15 is the birthday of Dr. Martin Luther King, Jr.

Supplies: Old cotton sheets or any white cotton fabric cut in 12-inch squares
Potatoes and/or styrofoam meat trays to print with
Cardboard
Needles and thread
Acrylic paints and brushes
Fabric dyes (optional)

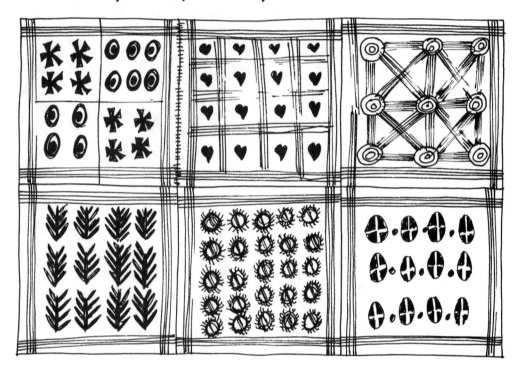

Procedure: Adinkra cloth is beautiful hand-stamped fabric made in Ghana. Simple symbols are used in repetitive patterns, each symbol having a special meaning. Examples of Adinkra cloth and background information on the symbols and their meanings should be provided for the students. First, cut old cotton sheeting into 12-inch by 12-inch squares (one for each student). If this is impractical, the prints could be done on paper and taped together. To make the prints, a potato stamp or a stamp

Adinkra prints (cont'd.)

made from a styrofoam meat tray will work quite well. If potatoes are used, cut them into 3/4-inch slabs. The slabs can be cut into simple shapes with table knives or scissor points. If styrofoam trays are used, they can be cut into shapes with scissors and details inscribed with pencil points. Place the square of cloth on some layers of newspaper. Make the squared off lines by painting the edge of a piece of cardboard with acrylic paint and stamping this on the fabric. Now brush acrylic paint onto the potato or styrofoam print and stamp the design in an orderly fashion onto the fabric. The stamp will need to be repainted after each impression. When the fabric is completely dry it can be dyed. All of the squares can be dyed the same color or in a variety of colors. Cold water fabric dye will be the most convenient way to approach this.

To make a large wall hanging, the fabric squares can be sewn together by machine or by hand.

Origami

Supplies: Paper (brightly colored if possible)

Drinking Cup

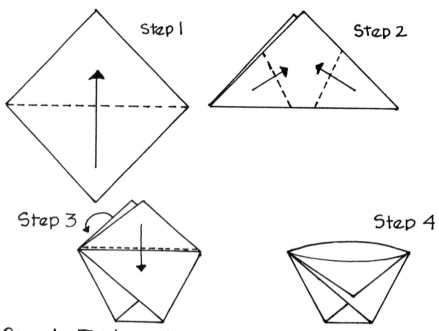

Procedure: Step 1: Fold the bottom corner up to the top corner. Step 2: Fold the right and left corners inward. Step 3: Fold the top two corners down on either side of the cup. Step 4: The cup is finished. It will actually hold cold liquids for a short time.

The House

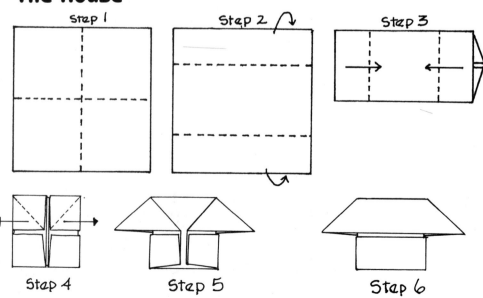

Step 1: Fold the paper into quarters. Step 2: Fold the top and bottom edges down so that they meet at the center fold in the back. Step 3: Fold the left and right edges in so they meet at the center line in front. Step 4: To make the roof, pull the two upper flaps in an outward direction. Flatten them as shown in step 5. Step 5: The house is finished; turn it over. Step 6: Front view is shown. Now draw in windows and doors.

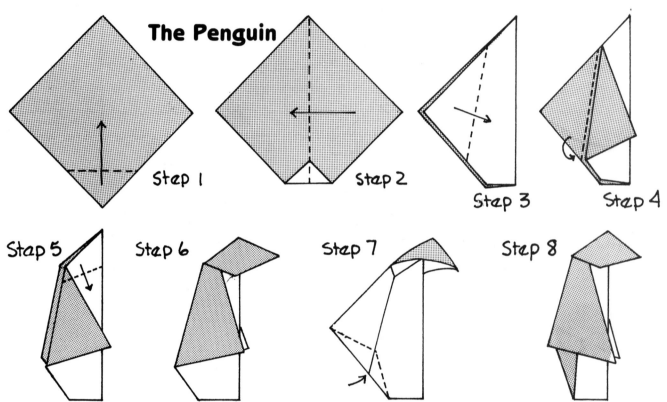

The Penguin

Step 1
Step 2
Step 3
Step 4
Step 5
Step 6
Step 7
Step 8

If possible, use paper that's dark on one side and white on the other. If not, color one side of white paper. Step 1: With dark side up, fold up the bottom corner. Step 2: Fold right corner inward to left corner. Step 3: To make the first wing, fold the left flap forward so it extends a bit past the center fold. Step 4: Make the second wing the same way. Step 5: Make the head by folding the top flap forward; then unfold it. Unfold the center fold slightly and pull up and out. It will form a hood-like shape. Step 6: Step 5 is completed. Step 7: Finish the wings by opening them up and fold in as shown. Step 8: The penguin is finished.

Snowman Pendants

Supplies: Flour, salt, water
Oven
Acrylic paint, brushes
Paper clips or flexible wire, ribbon or string
Polyurethane varnish

Use a pencil point to poke holes for mouths and belly buttons.

Procedure: Use the baker's clay recipe found on page 75. This will be enough for 6 or 7 snowman (or lady) pendants. Make the pendants small, about 1½ to 2 inches high. This will cut down on baking time. Roll small spheres for the torso, head, feet, nose, ears, and pompons. The arms are cylindrical shapes and the hat can be formed from a cone shape bent over to one side. Join the body parts together securely, using a little bit of water for slip. Insert a paper clip or a wire loop into the hat. Bake the sculptures in a 350° oven until they're completely dry (about an hour). Then paint them evenly, using acrylic paints. When the paint is dry, dip the figures in polyurethane varnish. This will add gloss and protect them from moisture. When the varnish is dry, thread the pendant with a ribbon.

Baker's Clay Candleholders

Supplies: Flour, salt, water
Mixing bowls, rolling pin
Cardboard tubes (Pringle's cans, paper
  towel cardboards, etc.), aluminum foil
Oven

Procedure: Stir 4 cups of flour, 1 cup of salt, and 1½ cups
of water together in a large bowl. This is
enough dough for one or two castles. Knead the
mixture for approximately 10 minutes on a
lightly floured surface. The dough should be
smooth and pliable. (If the dough must be
stored, put it in a plastic bag and store it in
the refrigerator.) Roll the dough to the
desired thickness (¼ inch or less). Cover
an assortment of cardboard tubes with foil
and wrap the dough around them, smoothing
out the seam. Put a base on the turret.
Decorate the candleholder by punching interesting designs into the dough. Holes must be
provided at the bottom and top for circu-
lation. Tops for the turrets should be made to
fit separately. Bake for several hours at
350°.

Candle Dipping

Supplies: 2 32-ounce juice cans
A two-burner hot plate
Cooking oil
2 large saucepans
8-10 16-ounce boxes unrefined paraffin
Wire coat hangers (one or two per student)
Medium-sized candlewick
2 coordinating colors of wax crayons
   (red/yellow, yellow/green, blue/purple)
Scissors

Procedure: Clean the cans inside and out and wipe with a coat of cooking oil. Place the cans in 3 to 4 inches of water in the saucepans. Cut the paraffin into small chunks and place the chunks in the cans. Turn on the hot plate and heat the water to boiling. Allow the wax to melt. There should be enough wax in the containers to fill the cans one inch below the rim. Keep the water at a low boil. While the wax is melting you can prepare the candle dippers. Bend the hangers as shown on the next page and tie on the wicks. When the wax is melted, take the paper off the crayons and drop them into the cans to color the wax. When

candle dipping (cont'd.)

the crayon is mixed in, turn off the burner and let the wax cool slightly. Dip the wire frames and wicks into the wax up to within an inch of the wick end. Hang them up until the wax hardens. As the wax in the cans cools, a shorter solidifying time will be required. Just dip and hold the frame over the can for a few moments, then dip again. About half an hour of repeated dipping will complete the candles. Hang the frames up for the final drying period - about an hour or until the wax is firm. With scissors cut the wick at the top and bottom and free the candles from the frame. Scrape the wax off the frames back into the cans to reuse.

The remaining liquid wax can be turned into candles by putting the cans into the refrigerator for the wax to harden. Then remove the wax from the cans by putting the cans in hot water. To add the wicks, heat a straight piece of wire coat hanger and push it all the way through the middle of the candle. Now insert the wick into this hole, pushing it through with the straightened coat hanger. Seal the opening with some melted wax.

January Bulletin Board Idea

Supplies: Colored construction paper
Pins or tacks
String or yarn
Brightly colored background paper
Scissors
Markers
Party horns or streamers (if you have them

Procedure: Pin or staple a brightly colored background paper onto the bulletin board. Cut the letters from colored construction paper. Cut out a pattern for a balloon that you can draw around. Make enough so that each student will have one balloon on which to write his/her New Year's resolution. Punch a hole in the bottom of each balloon and thread a string through the hole. Pin or tack the balloons up to the bulletin board.

"I'm done already!" Cards

Productive time-fillers for those who finish first.

January

Self-Portrait

January

You'll need a large sheet of paper, a hand mirror, pencil, crayons, or paint. Look into the mirror and sketch a likeness of yourself. Color it in with crayons or paint.

Coasters

Collect 6 Pringles can lids. Paint a design on the inside of each of the lids with acrylic paint. Spray with clear acrylic spray if desired.

Decorated Bottle

January

Find a bottle with an interesting shape. Cut squares or small pieces from colored construction paper or colored magazine pages. Paste them on the bottle in a mosaic pattern. Spray with clear acrylic spray when dry.

Cookbook Bookmark

January

Use a wooden spoon as a pattern and cut the bookmark from colored felt. Decorate the bookmark with sequins or glitter and tie a tassel onto the end.

"I'm done already!" Cards

Productive time-fillers for those who finish first.

Spool Prints

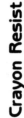

With white glue, glue a length of string in a random pattern onto a spool or dowel. Let the glue dry. Paint the spool with tempera paint and roll the spool in different directions across a piece of paper.

Crayon Resist

Take a white crayon and draw a picture on a piece of paper. Brush dark watercolors over the paper and your picture will suddenly appear. Add the details with crayons or felt tip pens.

Invisible Ink

Use lemon juice to draw a picture or write a secret letter to a friend. Your message will only become visible when the paper is heated by holding it over a light bulb or pressing it with an iron.

Pencil Holder

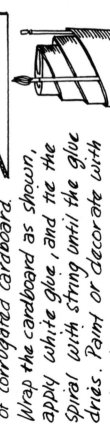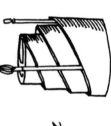

Cut a triangle from a piece of corrugated cardboard. Wrap the cardboard as shown, apply white glue, and tie the spiral with string until the glue dries. Paint or decorate with colored paper.

80

February

Arts & Crafts
Valentine Sachets

4" FOLD

2½"

Supplies: Two pieces of red or red print fabric (4" x 5") per project
More fabric scraps for "appliques"
Twelve to sixteen inches of 1" ribbon per project
Pins, needles, red thread, glue, scissors
Cotton balls
Paper to cut patterns
Scented bath powder or inexpensive cologne

Procedure: Cut a few heart patterns as illustrated above. Using the paper pattern, cut 2 hearts from red or red print fabric. Cut hearts or other designs from fabric scraps and glue them to the heart. Pin the two hearts together and sew them using a simple running stitch. Leave a 2" opening. Roll a handful of cotton balls in the scented powder or spray them with cologne. Insert the cotton balls into the 2" opening on the heart and sew up the opening. Make a bow with the 1" ribbon and sew it at the top of the heart.

Wooly Groundhog

Supplies: Sturdy cardboard
Scissors
Yarn (brown, camel and black) 1 oz. of each
Buttons (for eyes)
String
Needles and thread

Sew on a piece of felt for a tail.

Procedure: Cut the pattern that is shown on the opposite side out of sturdy cardboard. Now begin winding the yarn around the pattern. Begin winding at the nose end of the cardboard and make 100 wraps of the brown yarn along the pattern in the area between the dotted lines. It is very important that the winding be done in even layers, so start at one end of the card, and wind the wool evenly to the other end, and then back to the starting point and so on. When the head is wound, the rest of the body can be wound, using brown, camel and black yarn. Time can be saved by winding the three colors at the same time, making 200 wraps with the three-fold yarn. The winding should all be done loosely so that there is no chance of bending the cardboard. In beginning to wind, the first loose ends are secured by winding over them.

wooly groundhog (cont'd.)

If a new length of yarn needs to be started, there is no need to join the ends. The next step is to wrap a length of string twice around the yarn inside the center slit. The ends of the cord are overlapped for about 3/4 inch and sewn together with needle and thread. Make the overlap near the center as shown below. The cords on both sides of the yarn are then sewn together firmly, passing to and fro through the slit. The

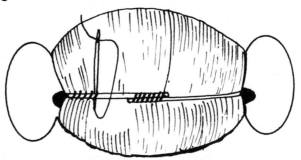

stitches should be about 1/8 inch apart and when the end is reached, the cords should be sewn together again in the other direction. Now cut the wool at the edge of the cardboard with scissors, cutting two or three layers at a time. Now shape the animal by trimming the sides and underside. (See cutaway view.) Make the nose with a few stitches of black yarn. Sew the buttons together for eyes about 1 inch from the tip of the nose by passing the needle from side to side of the nose.

½ ACTUAL SIZE

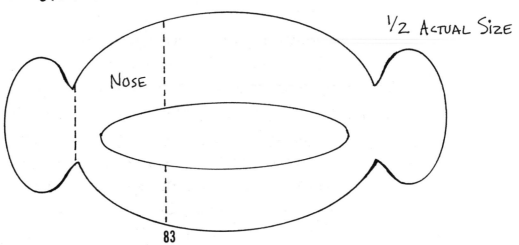

NOSE

Star Weaving

Supplies: Sticks or dowels (enough for 2 sticks per student)
Plenty of brightly colored yarn (at least 2-ply)

Figure 1
Lashing

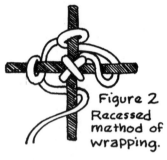

Figure 2
Recessed
method of
wrapping.

Figure 3
Raised
method of
wrapping.

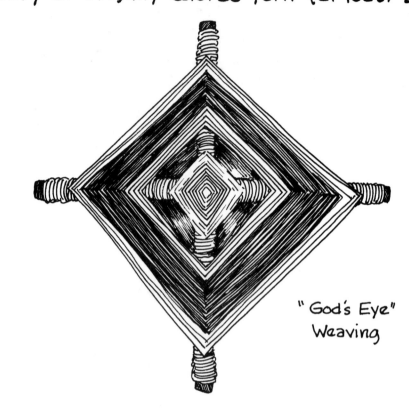

"God's Eye"
Weaving

Figure 4
Joining a new
color.

Procedure:

Lay 2 sticks of approximately the same length at right angles. Lash the 2 sticks together with yarn as shown in figure 1, winding the yarn around in a "figure 8" pattern until the center wood is completely covered. Tie a knot on the backside of the sticks using the original tail of the yarn and the yarn you now hold in your hand. Do not cut the yarn. Begin weaving with this yarn using one of the two methods shown in figures 2 and 3, the recessed method or the raised method. In both cases, all of the wood is covered until the ends of the sticks are reached. Changing colors is easily managed by joining the colors with a knot on the backside of the star as shown in figure 4. Finish the star by tying a knot on the back of the star. Make certain all knots are tight and trimmed.

Valentine Pins

Supplies: 7-10 loaves of white bread (enough for 8 slices per student)
White glue (enough for ½ cup per student)
Shellac or glossy polymer medium
Poster paints or acrylic paints
India ink and pens
¼ inch wide, brightly colored satin ribbon
Small gold safety pins

Procedure: The sculpting material for this project is bread clay. To make one recipe of bread clay, the crusts from 8 slices of white bread must be removed. Tear the slices into small pieces and combine with ½ cup white glue, adding a little glycerin if desired. The ingredients must be mixed for 5 minutes or so, until the stickiness is gone. If colored dough is desired, add poster paints or acrylic paints directly to the dough, kneading until the color is worked through. Make the pins by shaping the dough into the desired shapes, then poke a hole near the top through which to string the ribbon when the piece is dry. Air-dry the pieces for a couple of days. Add details with acrylic paints and India ink, then shellac the piece and again allow to dry, string a brightly colored ¼ inch satin ribbon through the top and pin on a small gold safety pin.

Valentine Pop-ups

Supplies: Paper (colored and white)
Scissors
Rubber cement
Crayons
Paints
Markers

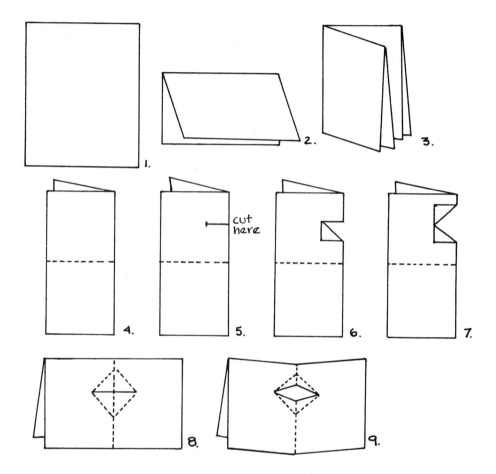

Procedure: In order to understand how to make a pop-up card, use the drawings above and the steps below to make a simple pop-up card. This basic technique will make it easy to create all kinds of 3-dimensional effects. Take a piece of notebook paper and fold it in half, first horizontally, then vertically (figures 1,2 and 3). Open the card up completely and fold it vertically in the opposite direction (figure 4). Snip the card horizontally through the fold as shown in figure 5.

Valentine pop-ups (cont'd.)

Fold back the edges of the slit, thus making two right-angled triangles (figures 6 and 7). Fold the triangles forward and backward, in both directions, to make the paper flexible. Fold the card as shown in figure 8. Arrange the pop-up as shown in figure 9, so that when you close the card the pop-up is folded outward. Open and close the practice card several times until the pop-up suggests an idea for a picture.

Note to the Teacher: Now that the basic technique of making a pop-up is understood, you will want to make a couple of sample cards as a demonstration and encourage your students to elaborate on this technique and create their own pop-ups. A few sample ideas are pictured below.

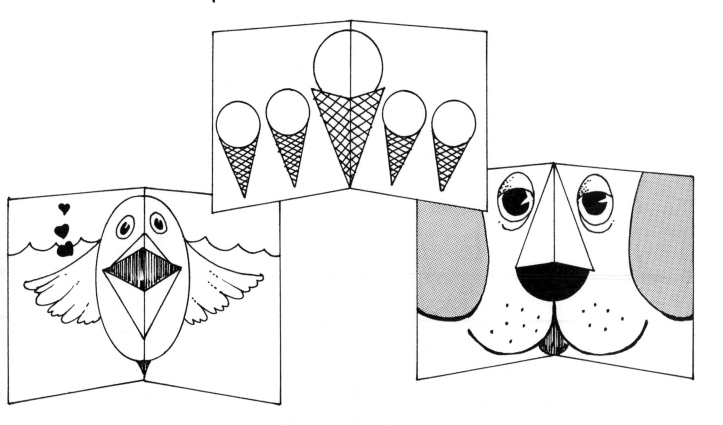

Tribal Masks
February 21st is Malcolm X Day.

Supplies: Lots of old newspapers
Scissors or paper cutter
Wheat paste, library paste or wallpaper paste
 thinned to the consistency of cream
Something to mix the paste in (perhaps
 plastic milk jugs with the tops cut off)
Various objects to use as armatures (boxes,
 balloons, crumpled newspaper, bowls, etc.)
Sandpaper
Acrylic or tempera paint and brushes
Clear acrylic spray or shellac
Yarn, feathers, fabric scraps, etc.

Note to the Teacher: Provide plenty of pictures of primitive African art and tribal masks and costumes to give the students a good feel for the art form.

Procedure: Tear or cut the newspapers into ½-inch-wide strips. Mix the paste with water until it is the consistency of cream.

tribal masks (cont'd.)

After drawing a sketch of the mask you wish to create, decide which objects will make the best armature for the desired shape. Lay these out on some newspapers. Lay the first layer of strips paste side up, so that the mask will come off of the mold easily when it's dry. The first layer of strips should be placed on the mold in a star-like pattern, the second layer parallel to your body and the third at a right angle to that. The fourth and fifth layers should be placed at opposing diagonals. This will make the construction firm. Make sure all wrinkles

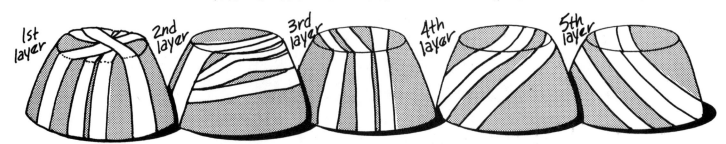

1st layer 2nd layer 3rd layer 4th layer 5th layer

and bubbles have been smoothed out before the next layer of strips is added. Continue to add strips until the entire armature is covered. Repeat until at least six layers of strips have been applied. Add features at this point (nose, cheeks, chin, etc.) by crumpling paper and laying more paper strips on top. Allow the papier-mâché to dry thoroughly and remove it from its armature. Cut holes for the eyes. Paint the features onto the mask with acrylic or poster paint. Now fasten other features or accessories in place with glue. Yarn, fabric scraps, and feathers can be used for hair, pebbles or corn kernels for teeth and so on. You may want to smooth the surface of the mask with sandpaper before painting. Spray the mask with clear acrylic spray or shellac for permanence.

Big Presidents

Supplies: A black and white picture of either George
Washington or Abraham Lincoln
Scissors
Pencils
White or manilla paper
Tape

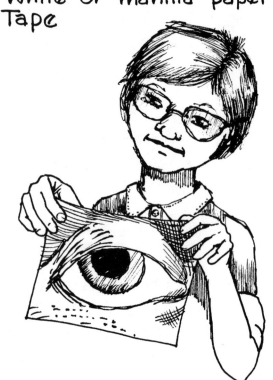

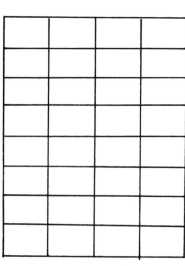

Cut the original picture
into equal parts.

Procedure: Take a black and white picture of either Abraham
Lincoln or George Washington and cut it into
enough pieces so that each student will get one
small piece of the portrait. All of the pieces
should be the same size. Now cut manilla or
white paper into proportionate size. For
example, if the small portrait pieces are 2
inches by 3 inches, the paper for the students
could be 8 inches by 12 inches. Now the individ-
ual pieces of the picture should be drawn with
pencil, as carefully as possible, proportion-
ately larger on the blank sheets of paper.
When all the students have completed their
drawings, rearrange the pieces, tape them
together on the backs and hang. The results
can be super!

Papermaking

Supplies: Old newspapers or paper towels (one newspaper page per student)
Wood strips, nails, hammer
Staple gun
Fine wire screen, a sponge
A blender or a big dishpan and an eggbeater
Dishwashing liquid or bleach
An iron, some pieces of an old sheet

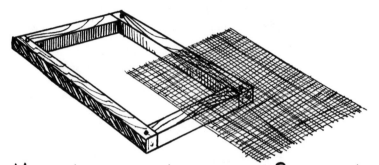

Procedure: Make two small wooden frames the same size (about 6 inches by 6 inches would work well). Staple wire screen to one frame. This will be called the mold. Tear up old newspaper or paper towels. Fill the blender ¾ full of warm water and tear up and add pieces of scrap paper until the liquid is cloudy but not thick. Hold the mold screen side up and place the empty frame on top. The empty frame is called the deckle. The deckle allows the water to drain slowly and forms the edges of the paper. Pour the paper liquid into a big dishpan. Dip both frames, with the screen "sandwiched" in the middle, into the dishpan. Raise the frames straight up from the dishpan and drain. Remove the top frame. Turn the screen over onto some folded fabric, sheet or paper towel blotter. Blot the back of the screen with a sponge to absorb excess moisture. Remove the screen. Put another blotter on top of the paper and iron dry. Remove blotters. Small objects like leaves and flowers can be embedded in the paper while still wet.

Printmaking

Supplies: Paper (manilla, colored, newsprint, etc.)
Water soluble printing ink
The rest of the supplies will vary according to the printing technique.

Inner Tube Prints

Procedure: You'll need: pieces of old inner tubes, scissors, heavy cardboard, white glue, brayers, and something to use for an ink slab. (A piece of glass with the edges taped will work well.) Cut shapes from the inner tube and glue them to the cardboard backing. Squeeze some ink onto the ink slab and roll it with a brayer until it is spread evenly. Roll the brayer over the design from side to side and top to bottom to make sure the ink is even. Place a piece of paper over the design and rub it with your fingers until the whole design has transferred to the paper. Re-ink the rubber design for each additional print.

Clothespin Prints

You'll need: a clothespin, a couple of small pieces of cardboard, white glue, scissors, and printing ink or tempera paint. Cut one small piece of cardboard and on it glue a design cut from another piece of cardboard. Glue these pieces to the end of a clothespin. Apply tempera paint to the raised area with a brush and stamp the design in a pattern on a piece of paper.

printmaking (cont'd.)

Potato Prints

You'll need: a potato, scratching tool, paring knife and tempera paint. Cut the potato in half, sketch a design and cut the background away.

All kinds of fruits and vegetables can be used successfully; carrots, cabbage, peppers, apples, turnips, etc.

Soap Prints

You'll need: a large bar of soap, a carving tool (nail file, knife, scissors, etc.) and tempera paint. Carve the design out of the soap and print.

String Prints

You'll need: a spool, string, white glue and printing ink or tempera paint. Glue the string on the spool in a predetermined pattern. Run a pencil through the middle hole for a handle. Roll the spool in tempera paint or printer's ink and print.

Eraser Prints

You'll need: an old eraser and some tempera paint or water soluble ink. Use the old eraser to print a repetitive pattern on paper. Either use one edge of the eraser to print with or carve a design into one side. Print as in the projects described above.

February Bulletin Board Idea

Supplies: White background paper.
Plenty of red construction paper
Pink construction paper and red or pink yarn
Scissors, tape, stapler
Markers

Procedure: Cover the bulletin board with white paper. Sketch the words, "Happy Valentine's Day!" lightly in pencil and cover the lettering with red or pink yarn. Each student should cut out two red hearts, about 10 inches wide, and lay one of the hearts down on a piece of pink construction paper. A scallop should be drawn about 1½ inches from the edge of the heart. Glue the bottom red heart to the pink paper and staple the top heart on. Label the hearts. Use these as your Valentine mailboxes.

"I'm done already!" Cards

Productive time-fillers for those who finish first.

Tin Can Containers

Decorate clean, dry tin cans by applying white glue to the can, small areas at a time. Wrap brightly colored yarn around the can while the glue is still wet. Use the can for pencils, rubber bands, bobbie pins or anything you want.

February

Toothpick Sculpture

Create an elaborate 3-dimensional sculpture using toothpicks and quick-drying glue. Glue the toothpicks together in a form of your choice.

February

Chalk Snapping

You can create a professional-looking abstract design with paper, chalk, string and a thumbtack. Push the tack into your drawing board and tie the the string to it. Rub the string with a piece of chalk. Put your paper under the string and pull the string down on top of the paper. Snap the string against the paper, moving the position of the paper several times. Now color the design.

February

Bathtub Sailboat

Make a bathtub sailboat for one of your brothers or sisters by cutting a milk carton in half as shown below. Open it up and insert a piece of cardboard for a sail as shown.

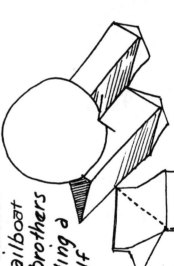

"I'm done already!" Cards

Productive time-fillers for those who finish first.

Valentine Collage

Make a collage of all the things you love. Take a piece of 8½" x 11" paper and glue on carefully chosen magazine pictures of the things that are precious to you.

Name Sculpture.

Use the Bread Clay recipe on page 85 to make one recipe of clay. Roll it out to a 1/8 inch thickness. Cut the letters of your name out of the clay and decorate your name as desired.

Popsicle Stick Trivet

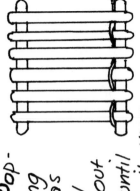

Make a trivet from Popsicle sticks by gluing 8 of them together as shown. Weave brightly colored yarn in and out of the Popsicle sticks until completely covered with yarn.

Color Explosion

You can create a color explosion that will take place before your very eyes! All you need is white, sturdy paper, water, and powdered fabric dyes. Wet the paper and lay it out on some newspapers. Sprinkle the powdered dye onto the wet paper and POW, a color explosion!

March

Arts & Crafts
Tie-Dyeing

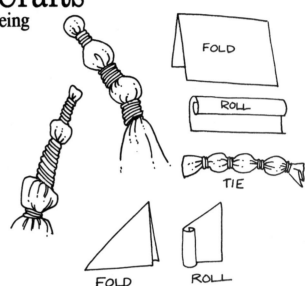

TIE-DYE
IS BACK AND
IT'S FUN TO DO!
TAKE ADVANTAGE OF ITS RENEWED POPULARITY
AND TEACH YOUR STUDENTS THIS AGE-OLD CRAFT!

Supplies: Fabric dye (lots of bright, springtime colors!)
Have each student bring an old, white T-shirt. You should probably
have some 36" square pieces of white cotton fabric for the
kids who don't bring a T-shirt. You can help them finish the
edges for a scarf or wall hanging.
String, rubber bands
Dishpans or big pots for dye

Procedure: Wrap and tie pieces of string or rubber bands in planned order all over
your T-shirt. Above are some illustrations that will help. Dip the
fabric into the pan of dye. You can use just one color, or dip some
knots in one color and other knots in another color. Carefully
wring out as much excess moisture as you can. Remove the
rubber bands and let it dry flat.

Springtime Stitchery

Supplies: Yarn (crewel yarn would be best, but heavier yarn will work well for a beginner)

Needles (large enough to thread with your selection of yarn)

Background material (linen twill, denim, burlap)

Scissors

Thimbles

Embroidery hoops (optional)

Procedure: Cut yarn lengths from 18 to 24 inches (a longer strand might get tangled or fray by the time you reach the end). Thread the needle and knot the yarn at the end. To start the yarn, bring the needle up through the bottom of the fabric so the knot will not show. When finishing a length of yarn, weave the thread under a few stitches on the wrong side and clip close to the fabric. On the following pages are directions for 11 stitches. Lightly sketch your springtime design on the fabric and fill it with stitchery.

Practice some of these stitches on fabric scraps before beginning your project.

Running Stitch

This is the simplest stitch. Just pass the needle in and out of the cloth on a straight or curved line. All stitches and spaces should be of a uniform length.

Threaded Running Stitch

After completing a length of running stitches, use a contrasting color of yarn to weave in and out of the stitches.

Whipped Running Stitch

After completing a length of running stitches, pass the yarn from right to left under each running stitch.

Couching Stitch

Lay several strands of yarn along the outline to be embroidered. At uniform intervals along the strands, bring the needle up on one side and down on the other side.

Stroke Stitch
Use this to form small designs. The stroke stitch is a large single stitch.

Back Stitch
Take one running stitch, pass the needle back down through the cloth right at the end of the running stitch, and bring it up at a distance twice as long as the length of the running stitch.

Chain Stitch

Bring the needle to the right side of the cloth. Make a loop of thread. Holding this loop down with the left thumb, take the needle down close to where it just came up and bring it to the right side of the cloth a short distance forward. Don't pull the thread tight. Then take the needle down just on the other side of the loop (to hold the loop and in place). Repeat the pattern.

Blanket Stitch

Used for edging hems, the blanket stitch is made by bringing the yarn to the front of the cloth, making a loop which is held under the left thumb, then making a running stitch to hold the loop in place.

French Knot

Keeping the needle point close to the cloth, wrap the yarn 2, 3, or 4 times (depending on the size of the knot desired) around the needle. Insert the needle close to where it came up. Pull the needle through to form the knot.

Satin Stitch

Use small running or back stitches to completely fill the design. This will act as padding so the finished work will stand in relief. The satin stitch is done in the opposite direction of the padding stitches and simply covers the padding with perfectly even, closely spaced stitches.

Cross Stitch

Make a series of diagonal stitches. Then work back across the stitches filling in the diagonals.

In Like a Lion!

Supplies: Rope (per student you will need: 12 inches of
1½-inch rope, 24 inches of ½-inch rope, and
10 inches of ³/₈-inch rope)
Manila twine (2 yards per student)
Felt scraps
6 pieces of 18-inch florist's wire per student

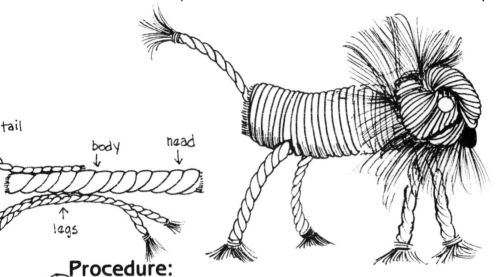

Procedure:

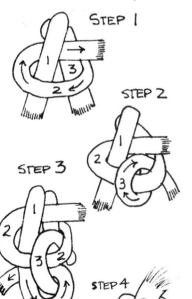

End of rope

STEP 1

STEP 2

STEP 3

STEP 4

felt scraps for eyes

— felt scrap for tongue

The rope can be easily shaped if you unwind
one strand from each piece of rope and replace
it with a piece of florist's wire). To make the legs,
cut the 24-inch piece of rope in half and wire
it. Tie the ends with a small piece of florist's
wire. To make the body and tail, lay the
length of 1½-inch rope and the ³/₈-inch rope
(wired) with the ³/₈-inch rope extending about 5
inches as shown in detail A. Wrap these together
with the Manila twine for about one inch. Then add
the two leg pieces and continue wrapping for
about 3 more inches and fasten with a knot. There
should be about 8 inches left of the 1½-inch
rope for the head. Unwind the 3 strands and
follow the sketches to the left to make the
head. Comb the excess rope out to make
the mane.

101

Paper Airplanes

Supplies: Paper (white typing or bond paper will work well)
Pencils, ruler
Stapler or paper clips
Colored markers

Design #1

Procedure: 1. Fold the sheet of paper in half lengthwise, making a sharp crease. 2. Unfold and crease lines "2u" so they meet in the middle. 3. Fold on lines "3u" so the edges again meet in the middle. 4. Fold "4d" to form the wings. 5. Fold on lines 5 to make stabilizers. 6. Put a staple or paper clip on the bottom about 1/3 of the way back from the nose.

"u" means fold the paper upward. "d" means fold the paper down.

Design #2

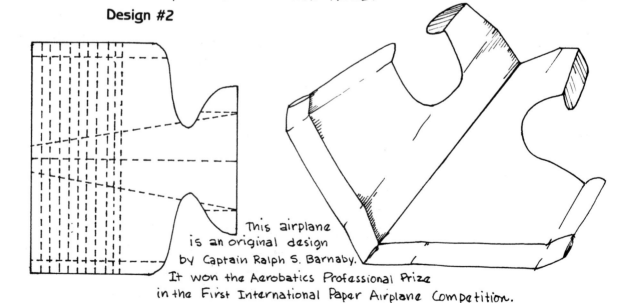

This airplane is an original design by Captain Ralph S. Barnaby. It won the Aerobatics Professional Prize in the First International Paper Airplane Competition.

paper airplanes (cont'd.)

Design #2

This plane is an acrobat. It performs glides, left and right turns, even returns to you, all depending upon small adjustments made in the wing tips and tail fins. Experimenting with wider or narrower folds in the wings and tail will also alter the flight characteristics. 1. Fold 8½x11 inch paper in half crosswise. 2. Make a series of nine ¼-inch folds, using half the sheet. 3. Fold along original crease again and cut along the solid line. 4. Fold the wings down on the creases to the side of the center crease. 5. Turn wing tips up and tail fins down.

Design #3

1. Fold the sheet in half crosswise. 2. Unfold and fold on line "2u," starting 1½ inches from the back. The corners should overlap the center line evenly. 3. Refold along the center line to fold overlaps, then fold on lines "3d." Add a staple or paper clip halfway along this "keel" to hold the folds together.

4. Fold down wing tips. 5. Form elevons by cutting lines "6" and folding up at a 45° angle (7u). 6. Fold back the nose on line 4 and add a paper clip.

Experiment with the flight pattern of this airplane by changing the position of the elevons, adding or removing paper clips from the nose, or changing the wing angles.

elevons

Note to the Teacher: If students want to decorate their paper airplanes, they should use colored markers or pencils. The paper can be decorated before the airplane is folded. This project in combination with _The Great Paper Airplane Factory_ by Becky and Charlie Daniel (also published by Good Apple) would make an excellent springtime unit.

"Easy as Pie" Rug Hooking

Supplies: Frame (wood "one by twos" nailed together)
Hammer and nails
A base on which to hook - burlap, gunny
   sack or rug canvas
A rug hooker, yarn, scissors
Thumbtacks or a staple gun

Procedure: Make a small frame (approximately 12
inches by 18 inches) by nailing strips of wood
together at the corners. The material is
stretched around the frame and stapled or
tacked to the back. Start at the center of one
side and move to the opposite side, then staple
the centers of each of the ends. After stretching
in this manner, tack or staple the material at
intervals of two inches from the centers out,
alternating sides of the frame. The design should
be drawn out on paper first, then cut out
and traced onto the burlap. If the frame is
too small for the design planned, several

rug hooking (cont'd.)

Pieces can be hooked and later sewn together to produce a bigger rug. Thread a rug hooker by pulling the yarn through the holes, leaving a tail of yarn 2 or 3 inches long projecting from the tip. Follow any special instructions enclosed with the particular hooker purchased.

Hold the frame with one hand or clamp it between two stationary objects. Working from the back, hold the needle perpendicular to the canvas as shown and push it through the cloth to the right side where the loop is formed. Pull the needle back. The loop remains in place. Push the needle through again, leaving a small space between each of the stitches. Continue making the loops, placing them in rows by moving back and forth across the canvas until each color area is filled. When the hooking is finished, the back of the rug may be sized with rug size or paint-on latex backing to hold the yarn securely in place. Remove the rug from the frame and trim the backing fabric border to one inch, and cut out the corners so the hem will not be bulky when turned under. Fold back the one-inch hem allowance, pin it in place, and stitch it to the rug with heavy duty thread.

Leprechaun Puppets

Supplies: Two 12-inch squares of felt for each body
Felt or fabric scraps for details and features
Black buttons or felt for eyes
White glue or fabric adhesive
Scissors
Needle and thread
Paper for the pattern

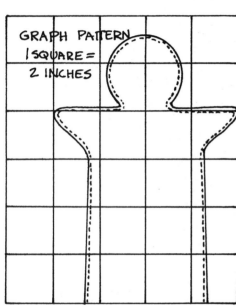

GRAPH PATTERN
1 SQUARE =
2 INCHES

Draw the pattern from the graph. One square equals two square inches.

Procedure: Cut out two leprechaun shapes. Cut the costume, hat, nose, buckles and buttons from felt or fabric scraps. Glue or sew them into position on one of the leprechaun shapes. Glue or sew the eyes into position. Sew the two halves of the puppet together, following the dotted line.

Note to the Teacher: If you don't have felt and have to use fabric for the body, sew the two sides together on the wrong side; turn. Iron and glue features.

106

Light-as-Air Balloons

Supplies: Balloons
Cotton embroidery thread or thin twine
White glue, waxed paper
Water

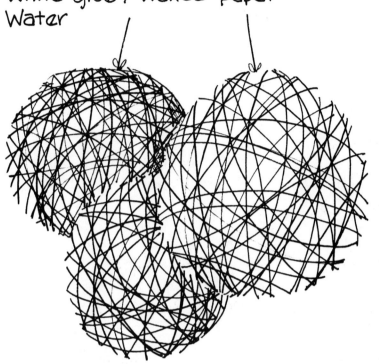

Procedure: Saturate the cotton embroidery thread or twine in a solution of 2/3 white glue and 1/3 water. Blow up a balloon to the size of a softball or cantaloupe. Draw the thread between the fingers and wrap it around the balloon. Allow the balloon to dry on waxed paper in a warm, dry place so the balloon does not shrink before the thread dries. When the thread is completely dry untie or pop the balloon. Remove it through one of the openings. Tie a string or a piece of fishing line to the top of the balloon and hang. Several of these prepared with different colored thread will make a beautiful springtime mobile.

March Bulletin Board Idea

Supplies: Colored background paper
Green construction paper (for shamrock)
Colored paper and markers

Procedure: Cover the bulletin board with a pale shade of background paper. Cut a shamrock shape out of green construction paper. (You may have to tape several sheets together from the back.) Draw a fairly complicated maze on it, first lightly with pencil, then with marker. Draw a simple lion and a simple lamb on paper, color them and cut them out. Cut the letters from black or dark green paper. Make a smaller duplicate of the shamrock maze to reproduce for each student.

"I'm done already!" Cards

Productive time-fillers for those who finish first.

Walking Spool

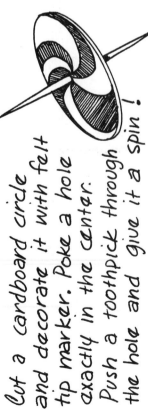

You need a rubber band, two toothpicks and a spool. Hold one toothpick steady and twist the other one until it's fairly tight. Let it go on the floor.

Private Catchall

Decorate an old lunch box with Contact paper, fabric scraps, yarn and permanent markers. Make it a special place for your private notes, extra change, sketches or poetry.

Spider Painting

For this project you will need a drinking straw, paper and ink or tempera paint. Drop a blob of ink or paint onto your paper. Now blow through the straw onto the paint and watch the paint spread into branch-like designs.

Spinning Top

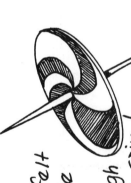

Cut a cardboard circle and decorate it with felt tip marker. Poke a hole exactly in the center. Push a toothpick through the hole and give it a spin!

109

"I'm done already!" Cards

Productive time-fillers for those who finish first.

Sand Painting

Take white sand or table salt and add food coloring to dye it. Mix each color in a separate container. Spread the mixtures out on paper plates and let them dry for an hour. To make your painting, lightly sketch your design on heavy paper. Spread white glue on all the areas to be the same color and sprinkle on the colored sand. Blow off the excess and save.

Brick Bookends or Doorstops

You can make your own bookends or doorstops by covering bricks with decorative paper or fabric or spray painting them. Add designs and details with felt, fabric scraps, pipe cleaners, acrylic paint, buttons, fun fur or yarn to match the colors of your room.

Long Bookmarks

Make yourself some super long, super special bookmarks, 15 or 20 inches long! Cut the shape of your choice out of felt or colored paper; add details with fabric scraps or felt tip marker.

Stacked Box People

Gather together boxes of various sizes and shapes. You'll also need plenty of materials to decorate the box person: colored paper, yarn, paints, gift wrap, etc. Glue the boxes and turn them into someone special!

April

Arts & Crafts
Easter Chicks

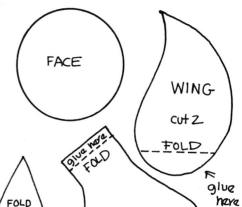

FACE

WING
cut 2
FOLD
glue here

glue here FOLD

FOLD BEAK
glue here

BODY

FEET
FOLD
FOLD
FOLD

Supplies: Sturdy yellow, green and orange
construction paper
Cotton balls, card board
Green powdered tempera paint
Scissors, glue, markers

Procedure: Use the patterns on this page to cut out the pieces of
your Easter chick. Cut everything but the beak and
feet from yellow paper. Cut the beak and feet
from orange paper. Fold where indicated and
assemble the chick with school glue. Cut a 4"
circle from cardboard and glue the chicks feet
to the circle. (See illustration.) Set the chick onto
the feet and put a drop of glue there to hold
the chick in place. Roll cotton balls in green tempera
powder and glue them onto the 4" circle surrounding
the chick.

glue
glue
glue

Spiral Breeze Catcher

Supplies: Colored construction paper or bristol board
Scissors, compass, ruler
String, glue

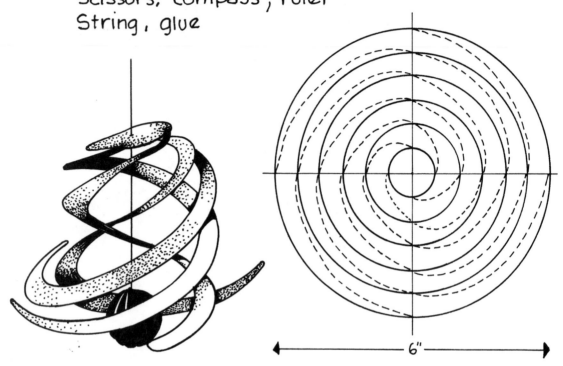

Procedure: Using a compass, draw a circle 6 inches in diameter. Then draw concentric circles ½ inch apart until you have drawn 6 circles (see sketch above). With a pencil and ruler, lightly divide the circle into 4 quarters. These are the guide-lines for drawing the spirals. Beginning in the center, draw the spirals as shown by the dotted lines in the sketch above. You will progress outward ½ inch per quarter turn. Cut around the outside circle and then cut the spirals carefully. Suspend a paper ball (see page 54 for instructions on how to make the ball) in the center and hang it by a thread. Put it up where there are air currents and it will spin constantly!

Spattered Leaf Designs
Arbor Day is usually celebrated in the spring.

Supplies: Tampera paints
Interestingly shaped leaves
Drawing paper
Small pieces of window screen
Old toothbrushes
Rubber cement or pins
Newspapers and tape

Procedure: Pin or rubber cement interestingly shaped leaves and plants to a piece of drawing paper. Fasten the drawing paper to the middle of some old newspapers with a piece of tape. Pick up a small amount of paint with the toothbrush. Hold the screen above the paper and rub the toothbrush back and forth across it, producing a fine spatter of paint. When the paint is dry, remove the leaves and rub off the excess rubber cement.

April

Spring Fabric Collage

Supplies: 1 piece of cardboard for each student
A wide variety of fabrics
Heavy fabric for backing, an iron
Fabric adhesive or library paste
Paper, pencils, toothpicks, pins
Scissors, pinking shears (for interesting edges)
Scraps of yarn, thread, string, braid, beads,
   buttons for decoration

Procedure:

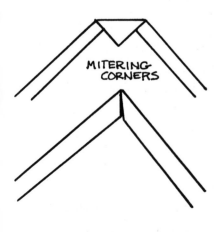

MITERING CORNERS

Apply a thin coat of fabric adhesive to the
sheet of cardboard. (Any glue or paste that will
not seep through and stain the fabric will work.)
Cover the cardboard with a sturdy fabric cut
slightly larger than the board. Miter the corners
and glue the raw edges to the back of the cardboard. Sketch out the design on a piece of
paper the same size as the cardboard. Cut out
these shapes and use them as patterns. Cut
the shapes from a variety of fabrics. If the
pieces are wrinkled, press them. Pin the
pieces onto the backing fabric into position. Use
a toothpick to dot the glue onto small areas
of the fabric. Add decorations or a border.

Papier-mâché Rabbit

Supplies: Balloons
Newspapers or paper towels
Scissors, pieces of cardboard to lay down
Wheat paste mixed with water to the consis-
   tency of cream
Sandpaper, tape
Paint (tempera or acrylic) and brushes
Clear acrylic spray
Cotton balls

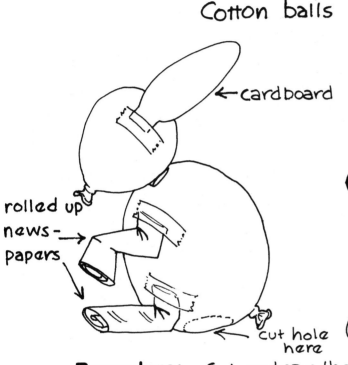

←cardboard

rolled up news-papers

cut hole here

Procedure: Cut or tear the newspapers into ½" strips. Mix the wheat paste. In-flate the balloons as shown: one about the size of a tennis ball, one the size of a small canta-loupe. Attach them with a piece of tape. Tape on ears and legs. Dip the newspaper strips into the paste. Drape the strips carefully over the armature until it is completely covered. Repeat until 6 layers have been applied (except ears, where only 2 layers are needed.) When the rabbit is dry, cut a hole as shown for inside to dry completely. Paint with tempera or acrylics and spray with acrylic spray.

Decorated Eggs

Supplies: Eggs (raw or blown)
Other supplies will vary according to the technique used.

Procedure: Eggs to be decorated can be left raw or emptied by blowing.
Blown eggs will be safer for students to work with. To blow an egg, pierce a hole in both the top and bottom of the egg and insert a needle to break the yolk. Shake the egg to mix the yellow and white together. Place the egg over a bowl and blow through the top hole until the contents have been emptied. Rinse with a mouthful of fresh water. Bake the shells in a 200° oven for 10 to 15 minutes to dry the egg and harden any yolk which could seep out later and spoil the design.

Tissue Paper Eggs

Supplies: Eggs, colored tissue paper, clear acrylic varnish or lacquer, paintbrushes, scissors, egg cartons and pipe cleaners

Procedure: Decide on a design or pattern for the egg to be decorated. Blow the egg. Cut the designs from brightly colored tissue. Several designs can be cut at once if small pieces of tissue are stacked together, stapled and then cut. Use clear acrylic glaze or lacquer to apply the tissue paper shapes. Brush on a little glaze, pick up the shape with the brush and set it in position on the egg. Brush a thin coat of glaze on top of the shape. Follow this procedure until the egg is complete. Brush on a final coat of acrylic varnish. Dry the egg by poking holes in egg cartons as shown. Put a pipe cleaner in each hole and place the egg on the pipe cleaner.

Egg Decals

Supplies: Blown eggs, white glue, colored magazine pictures or gift wrap paper, water, and paintbrushes

Procedure: Choose a small picture from a magazine or catalog and coat it several times with white glue. After the coats of glue have completely dried, soak the print in warm water and place it face down on a smooth countertop or desk. The colored ink will have been absorbed by the white glue, so the paper can be gently rubbed away, leaving a clear decal. Let the decal dry and carefully trim it to within 1/8 inch of the picture. Paint the surface of the egg with a coat of white glue. Smooth the decal onto the egg and coat once more with glue. Give the egg a final coat of polymer medium or lacquer.

Rubber Cement Resist Eggs

Supplies: Blown eggs, vinegar, rubber cement and dyes (either food coloring or homemade dyes as explained on page 119)

Procedure: Handle the eggs very gently since scratches and even fingerprints can show up when the egg is dyed. The egg can be held with a tissue while blowing or cleaned with a vinegar and water solution or patted with a soft cloth dipped in vinegar. First

decorated eggs (cont'd.)

dye the eggs with a light color, then dribble with the rubber cement in a random pattern. Let the cement dry. Dye the egg in a darker, contrasting color. Remove the egg from the dye and pat dry. Peel off the rubber cement and the design is revealed. (Blown eggs can be filled with water to weight them for dying.)

Plant Resist Eggs

Supplies: Blown or hard-boiled eggs to be eaten later, nylon stockings, leaves and flowers with distinct silhouettes, food coloring, rubber bands or freezer ties.

Procedure: Pick small plants or flowers with distinct outlines. If the plant is too stiff to drape over the egg, dip it in hot water to make it limp. Hold the plant against the egg, then wrap it tightly in a square of nylon stocking. Secure the nylon stocking with a rubber band or freezer tie. Submerse in food dye until the desired color is reached.

Scratch Eggs

Supplies: Blown eggs, dye, penknives or X-acto knives, clear acrylic spray

Procedure: First dye the egg, then lightly sketch a design on the dyed egg. Hold the egg in one hand with a paper towel or tissue and scrape away the dye over your design until the white is revealed. Work gently to avoid breaking the egg.

Drawing or Painting on Eggs

Supplies: Blown eggs, any kind of pen, marker or paint, clear acrylic spray or lacquer

Procedure: Draw or paint designs on the eggs and glaze with acrylic spray or lacquer.

Colors from Nature
Great for eggs, tie dye or batik!

Supplies: Enamelware pans
A hot plate or stove
Natural plant materials as listed below
Alum, salt, vinegar or cream of tartar

Procedure: Natural dyes are generally made by boiling plant substances in water to cover until the color is extracted. Any plant which stains the hands or clothing can be experimented with. To help the dye "take", experiment with alum, salt, vinegar or cream of tartar. In the chart below, the resulting color is assuming the use of alum.

Plant Form	Color
Acorns	Tan
Onion skins	Warm yellow to brown
Crab apples	Pink
Black walnut husks	Dark brown to black
Spinach, carrot tops, lily of the valley	Yellow-green to green
Beets, beet juice	Pink to wine
Grape juice	Steel gray
Clay	Tan-red brown
Cockleburs	Brass, dark green
Coffee grounds	Tan
Dandelion flowers	Yellow
Red cabbage leaves	Aqua
Goldenrod	Gray-green
Grapes (wild or concord)	Lavender
Lichen, oak	Pink-magenta
Marigold	Yellow-gold
Mulberry	Gray-lavender
Osage orange	Yellow-tan
Huckleberries	Purple
Sagebrush	Bright yellow
Sassafras	Red-tan

Paper Flowers

Supplies: Duplex (double thick) crepe paper in springtime colors
Duplex green crepe paper
18 gauge wire for stems
Bead wire in spools
Green florist's tape
White glue or paste

Tulips

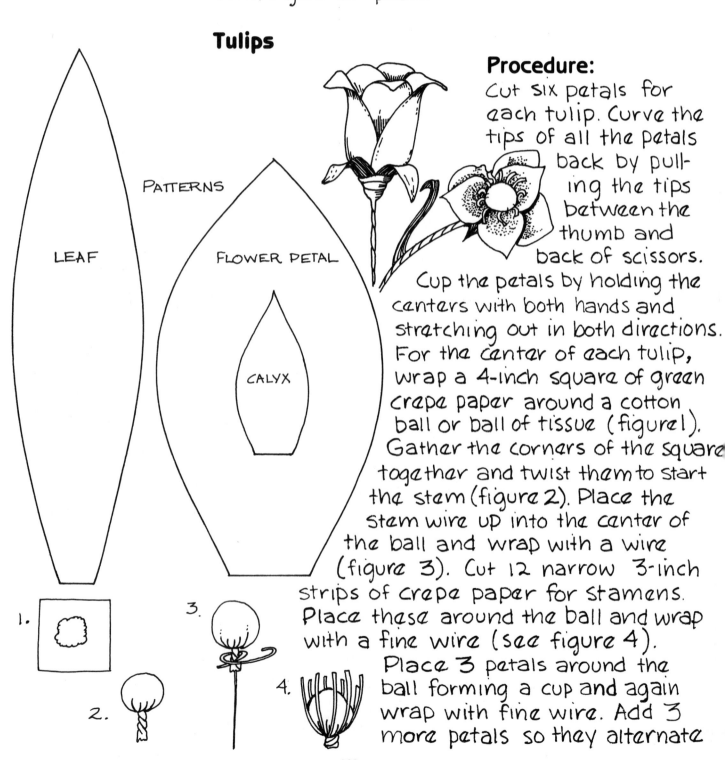

PATTERNS

LEAF

FLOWER PETAL

CALYX

1.

2.

3.

4.

Procedure:
Cut six petals for each tulip. Curve the tips of all the petals back by pulling the tips between the thumb and back of scissors.
Cup the petals by holding the centers with both hands and stretching out in both directions. For the center of each tulip, wrap a 4-inch square of green crepe paper around a cotton ball or ball of tissue (figure 1). Gather the corners of the square together and twist them to start the stem (figure 2). Place the stem wire up into the center of the ball and wrap with a wire (figure 3). Cut 12 narrow 3-inch strips of crepe paper for stamens. Place these around the ball and wrap with a fine wire (see figure 4).
Place 3 petals around the ball forming a cup and again wrap with fine wire. Add 3 more petals so they alternate

with the first three and wire in place. If the flower is too open, glue the edges of the outside petals to the inside petals. Add 3 green calyx to the bottom of the flower and tape into place. Tape the stem and add green leaves while taping.

Iris

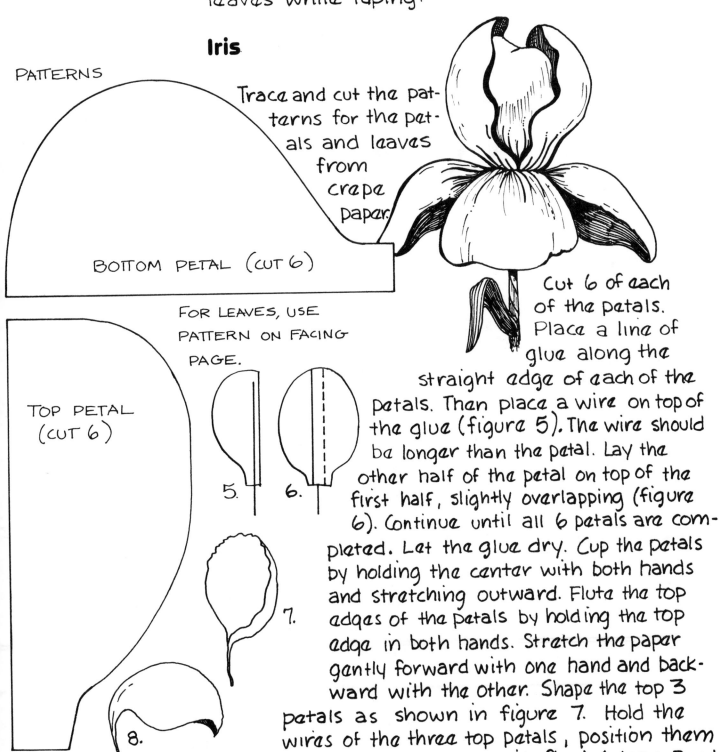

PATTERNS

Trace and cut the patterns for the petals and leaves from crepe paper.

BOTTOM PETAL (CUT 6)

FOR LEAVES, USE PATTERN ON FACING PAGE.

TOP PETAL (CUT 6)

5.

6.

7.

8.

Cut 6 of each of the petals. Place a line of glue along the straight edge of each of the petals. Then place a wire on top of the glue (figure 5). The wire should be longer than the petal. Lay the other half of the petal on top of the first half, slightly overlapping (figure 6). Continue until all 6 petals are completed. Let the glue dry. Cup the petals by holding the center with both hands and stretching outward. Flute the top edges of the petals by holding the top edge in both hands. Stretch the paper gently forward with one hand and backward with the other. Shape the top 3 petals as shown in figure 7. Hold the wires of the three top petals, position them in a cup shape and tape them together with florist's tape. Bend the bottom 3 petals as shown in figure 8. Place these around the bottom of the top 3 petals. Fasten with floral tape. Add stem wire & leaves.

April Bulletin Board Idea

Supplies: Colored background paper
Colored construction paper
Scissors
Stapler, tacks or pins
Markers or crayons

Procedure: Cover the board with colorful background paper. Cut out the letters and simple Jack-in-the-box shapes from colored construction or butcher paper. Cut 4-inch by 8-inch rectangles from colored paper. Fold in half. Write the riddle questions on the outside and the answers on the inside. Have each of the students do one of his/her own jokes. Staple the jokes up to the bulletin board. Change the jokes frequently during the month of April.

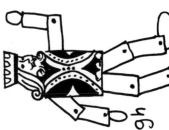

"I'm done already!" Cards

Productive time-fillers for those who finish first.

Homemade Spin Painting

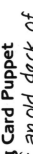

Poke a stick or a dowel through the bottom half of a one-gallon milk carton. Be sure the carton spins freely on the stick. Cut a piece of paper to fit the bottom of the carton and push it down over the stick. Spin with one hand and drop paint onto the paper.

| the carton
| the paper.

Mysterious Letters

Go through old magazines and newspapers. Cut out words, letters and pictures that will help you to assemble a letter, message or poster to give to a friend. Perhaps you would prefer to assemble the words to your favorite song or poem. Glue the words down to colored paper.

Playing Card Puppet

Using pieces of an old deck of playing cards for body parts, make a dancing puppet. Join the parts with paper fasteners through punched holes, and tie a string through the top.

Baby-Sitter's Helper

Cut all sizes of geometric shapes - circles, ovals, triangles, squares, and rectangles - from colored construction paper. Keep the cutouts in a cigar box or some other container and take the box of shapes with you when you baby-sit. The children can arrange the shapes into various objects: people, cars, animals, etc.

"I'm done already!" Cards

Productive time-fillers for those who finish first.

Balancing Toy

Practice making a toy that has perfect balance. Assemble boxes or wooden or styrofoam blocks, dowels or sticks, toothpicks, clay balls or something else to function as weights.

Wind Chimes

Be creative and make a set of wind chimes for your backyard or to hang outside your bedroom window.

Balls, metal scraps, tin can lids, bamboo, shells and so on can all be threaded on nylon line.

Sidewalk Art

With colored chalk and a big imagination you can create your own springtime "happening" outdoors. Color giant flowers, sunbursts or whatever else comes to mind outdoors on the sidewalk.

Make a Bunny

Make a bunny from:

1. a blown egg,
2. construction paper for ears, eyes, nose, paws and other details,
3. toilet paper or paper towel cardboard roll,
4. cotton balls for tail.

124

May
Arts & Crafts

String Spools
for Springtime Nests

Supplies: Empty spools
String, thread

Procedure: Fill an empty spool with several pieces of string cut about 6" long. Thread a piece of string 8" long through the spool and hang it in a tree in a spot that will be accessible to birds (and easy for you to see, too). Now, enjoy watching the birds select pieces of string for their springtime nests!

May Vases

Make these instead of May baskets and fill them with the homemade flowers from page 120.

Supplies: Liquid dish soap containers or potato chip canisters (one per student)
Scissors, glue
Fabric scraps, braid, trim, glitter, yarn
Acrylic paint, markers
Acrylic polymer medium

Procedure: Wash and dry the container. Decorate it by glueing on scraps of yarn, braid, rickrack, fabric, glitter, buttons or whatever scrap material you have handy. If only fabric scraps are used, a final coat of polymer medium will help to give the "vase" a finished appearance. Fill with real or homemade flowers and use them for May baskets.

Here Comes the Sun!

Supplies: Butcher paper, colored or white
Construction paper
Hole punch
Key ring
Scotch tape or stapler
Scissors, Glue
Colored markers or crayons

Procedure: Unroll a 25-foot length of butcher paper and cut it 18 inches wide. Double it over so it's 12½ feet long. Now start at one end and accordion pleat it carefully. With markers or crayons, color the pleats orange and yellow, alternately. When this is done punch a hole in one end through all the layers and insert a key ring. Open the sunburst and tape or staple the ends together. Glue a construction paper circle with a smiling face in the center. Facial details (eyelashes, lips) can be made from construction paper.

Note to the Teacher: This project can be varied in many ways. If you wish to make it smaller, decrease the width and length of the paper. For another variation on this project, you could use Paper Towel Dip'n Dye (p.128) or see the Giant Wall Star on p. 51.

Dip 'n Dye

Supplies: Food dye (The institutional kind that comes in one-quart-sized bottles is the least expensive. You can get it through your school cafeteria.)

Unperforated, white paper toweling (the kind used in the crank-type dispensers)

Plastic liver containers (free from your butcher)

Scissors

Water

Procedure: Fill the plastic containers half full with water. Put in enough food dye to make an intense, dark solution. Cut strips of the paper toweling to various lengths. Fold the paper in different patterns and dip. The way the towel is folded determines the design on it. Unfold the paper and let dry completely.

Note to the Teacher: The strips of paper toweling can then be glued together along the edges and used for kites, gift wrap, room dividers, origami, or wall decoration.

Bubble Prints

Supplies: Food dye (The institutional kind that comes in one-quart-sized bottles is the least expensive. You can get it through the school cafeteria.)
Liquid dish soap
Plastic liver containers (free from your butcher)
Drinking straws
White paper

Procedure: Fill the plastic containers half full of water. Pour in plenty of food dye; the solution should be very intense. Squeeze in a little dish soap. Blow through a drinking straw into the solution until there is a 4-inch to 5-inch mound of bubbles. Lay the piece of white paper face down onto the mound of bubbles.

Note to the Teacher: Fill several containers with different colors of dye. Printing one color on top of another works well. Students can work into the bubble prints with pens or markers to create pictures. This paper can also be used for paper-folding projects throughout the book.

Kites

The Two-Stick Kite

Supplies: Kite sticks (Each student will need one 32-inch-long stick and one 36-inch-long stick)

Knives or fine saw blades

Scissors, glue

Big sheets of paper (This can be sheets of dip and dye paper glued together at the edges, butcher paper, crepe paper or newspaper.)

Supplies to decorate the kite

String

Fabric scraps or crepe paper streamers for a tail.

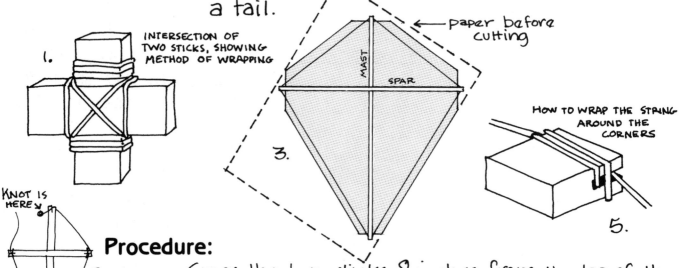

1. INTERSECTION OF TWO STICKS, SHOWING METHOD OF WRAPPING

← paper before cutting

MAST

SPAR

3.

HOW TO WRAP THE STRING AROUND THE CORNERS

5.

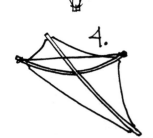

KNOT IS HERE

2.

4.

Procedure:

Cross the two sticks 8 inches from the top of the longer stick. Glue and lash as shown in figure 1. Cut notches in both ends of each stick. Put the string around the kite as shown in figure 2. Lay the kite on the paper and cut so there is one inch of extra paper around the string (figure 3). Fold the paper over the string and glue. Bow the cross bar 3 or 4 inches with a length of string (figure 4). Tie a string loosely from one end to the other of the cross bar. Do this on the front side of the kite. Tie a string from one end to the other of the longer stick. Again, tie it

130

kites (cont'd.)

loosely. Tie the two strings together where they meet. Now tie the main string to this junction. Make a tail from crepe paper, rags or fabric scraps. Attach it and the kite is ready to fly.

The Star Kite

Supplies: Kite sticks (Each student will need 3 sticks, 32 inches long.)
Paper (36 inches by 36 inches), string, glue

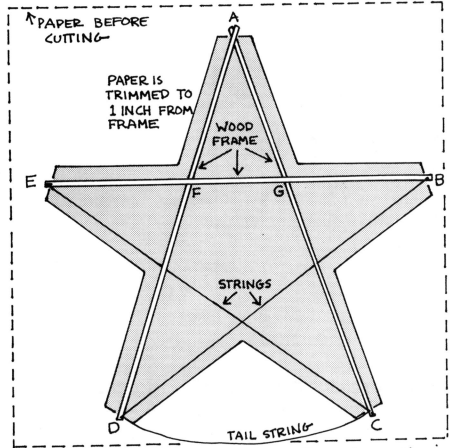

PAPER BEFORE CUTTING

PAPER IS TRIMMED TO 1 INCH FROM FRAME

WOOD FRAME

STRINGS

TAIL STRING

A
E
B
F
G
D
C

HOW TO CUT STICKS TO OVERLAP AT POINT A

6.

Procedure:

Cut the two sticks that will overlap at point A as shown in figure 6. Cut notches at points B, C, D, and E as shown in figure 5 on page 130. Match the two sticks at point A; measure 12½ inches down on both sticks from point A and mark those spots. Then measure and mark 11¾ inches from both ends of the cross stick. Line these marks up to form the frame. Glue and lash as shown in figure 1 on page 130. Run two strings from points B to D and C to E. Wrap and tie the strings as shown in figure 5 on page 130. Now lay the frame on the piece of paper and cut the paper one inch wider all the way around. Fold over and glue the edges. Tie two strings 48 inches long from D to A and C to A on the front side. Bring the strings together above the cross stick between F and G. Tie the flying string here.

Flower Blottos

Supplies: White paper
Colored construction paper
Tempera or acrylic paint
Scissors, glue

Procedure: Cut several rectangles of varying sizes from the white drawing paper. Fold each paper in the center and open it back up again. Drop some globs of tempera or acrylic on one side of the fold, refold the paper and press firmly. Open the paper and see the results -- interesting shapes that resemble all kinds of living things. Experiment with using more than one color. When several blottos have been made, cut them out and make a springtime collage from them. Mount the blottos and other design elements on a large piece of colored construction paper.

Tissue Creatures
Mobiles for gentle spring breezes

Supplies: Art tissue (brightly colored tissue paper)
Pencils
Scissors, glue
Facial tissues, toilet paper newspapers (for
   stuffing)
Sticks or dowels
Thread or fishing line

Cut two of
each shape

Procedure: Design several simple animals for the mobile. Draw the outlines of the animals on
pieces of brightly colored tissue paper. Lay
this pattern on top of another piece of tissue paper and cut two of each creature.
Glue the two pieces together by drizzling a
thin stream of glue along the edges, leaving
either the right or left side of the creature
open as shown in the sketch above. Let dry
completely and draw details with black or
colored ink.   Stuff them gently with crumpled
tissues, toilet paper or newspaper. Hang the
creatures by thread or fishing line, then hang
from sticks or dowels.

Summer Scrapbook

Supplies: Large sheets of sturdy, white paper
Cardboard
Cover material, fabric or decorated paper
Rulers
X-acto knives
Library paste or rubber cement
Paper towels, wax paper

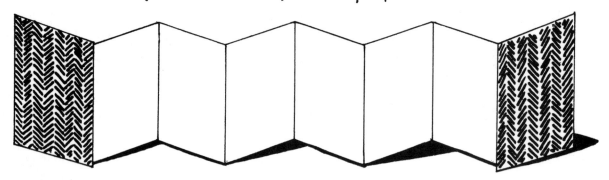

Procedure:

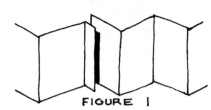

FIGURE 1

Take a long strip of paper and fold it first one way and then the other into consistently sized sections to form the pages of the book. If you want more pages and your paper is too short, leave a ½-inch tab at one end so you can paste the next section of pages to that (see figure 1). Now weight the pages under heavy books to keep the creases sharp and the pages flat. Cut two pieces of cardboard for the covers. They must be cut ⅛ of an inch larger than the pages on all four sides. Measure carefully to make certain that they are perfect rectangles and cut with an X-acto knife, paper cutter, or scissors. Now cut the outside cover material. Use either clean, pressed pieces of fabric for this, or use some of the printmaking or marbling techniques described earlier in this book to decorate pieces of paper. The cover must be cut 3/4 of an inch wider on all four sides than the pieces of cardboard (see

summer scrapbook (cont'd.)

FIGURE 2

FIGURE 3

FIGURE 4

FIGURE 5

figure 2). Smear paste evenly on the cardboard and lay the board down on the backside of the material. Smooth on both sides with a piece of clean paper towel. Cut the corners off of the cover material as shown in figure 3. Do not cut the corners flush to the corners of the board. Leave enough material to equal the thickness of the board. Now apply glue to these flaps of material. Fold them over and press them to the cardboard cover (see figure 4). To attach the cover to the pages, paste each of the end sheets of the folded sheet of paper to the backside of the cardboard cover (see figure 5). This becomes the lining sheet. If a more decorative lining is desired, it can be pasted over the end sheet that is pasted to the cardboard. Strips of colored paper, paper towel dip and dye, bubble printed sheets, or a summertime magazine collage are all optional lining sheets. Put wax paper inside of the cover sheets and weight the scrapbook under some heavy books for a couple of days until it's completely dry. Remove it from the weights and you have a perfect place to keep snapshots, poetry, postcards, lists, a diary or anything else that's important to you.

Stencil Pillows
Great for Mother's Day Gifts!

Supplies: Cotton duck cloth, canvas, or some other
sturdy, closely-woven fabric
Acrylic paint or fabric paint or paste fabric
dye
Stencil brushes
Poster board, X-acto knives or scissors
An iron
Masking tape
Needles, thread and pins
Fiber fill, old pantyhose or some other
kind of stuffing

Cut the fabric
twice as long as
the finished pillow
will be. For example,
if the finished pillow
is to be 12 inches by
12 inches, cut the
fabric 12 inches by
24 inches.

Procedure: Carefully choose a simple design and draw
it on poster board. With an X-acto knife or
scissors, cut the design out of the poster board.
Now lay the fabric out on a work surface. (Iron
out any wrinkles first.) Tape the stencil onto
the fabric with masking tape and put some of
the dye or paint into a shallow container. Dip
the stencil brush into the paint (don't get too
much paint on the brush) and brush the paint
gently over the stenciled area. Let this dry
a little and move to the next spot and continue until the piece of material is filled. Let
dry. Fold the fabric in the middle with right sides
together. Sew 2½ sides together; stuff and
sew the rest with a blind stitch.

136

Silhouettes
Great for Mother's Day Gifts!

Supplies: Large sheets of white drawing paper
A slide projector
Pencils
Black construction paper
Scissors, rubber cement

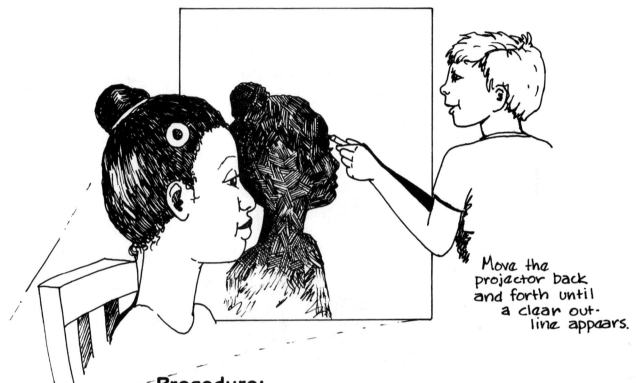

Move the projector back and forth until a clear outline appears.

Procedure:
Set up a projector about 10 feet from a wall. The subject should sit between the projector and the wall. Turn the projector light to on and tape a piece of large, white drawing paper so the subject's silhouette appears at the center of the sheet. Trace the contour of the profile carefully. Take the paper down and cut out the white silhouette. Lay it on a piece of black construction paper and trace around it. Cut this silhouette out and rubber cement it to a clean sheet of white drawing paper.

May Bulletin Board Idea

Supplies: Colored background paper
Drawing paper (12" x 18" sheets)
Colored construction paper
Scissors, stapler
Markers, crayons, pencils

Procedure: Cut 12 inch by 18 inch drawing paper into cloud shapes, one for each student. Have them draw, color, or paint a picture of how they plan to have fun over summer vacation. Meanwhile cover the bulletin board with brightly colored paper and staple it up. Cut out the simple circular shapes for the child's head and staple them to the board. Draw on the features. Pin or tack up the children's fantasies as shown.

"I'm done already!" Cards

Productive time-fillers for those who finish first.

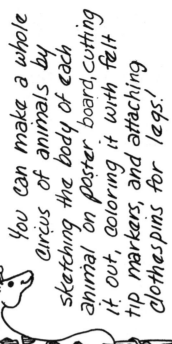

Make a Circus

You can make a whole circus of animals by sketching the body of each animal on poster board, cutting it out, coloring it with felt tip markers, and attaching clothespins for legs!

May

Springy Characters

Take a spiral wire from an old hair curler or spiral notebook and glue a cotton ball to one end. Stick the other end through an inverted paper cup, gluing and taping the wire inside the cup. Add any features you like to give your character its own special personality.

May

Sponge Painting

A regular kitchen sponge can add interesting texture to paintings. Dip one corner of your sponge into tempera or watercolor paint and use it in a blotting action. This kind of painting will make landscape and still life paintings.

May

Optical Whirlers

You can get the illusion of a lion jumping through a hoop by drawing a jumping lion on one side of a small piece of cardboard and a hoop on the other. Poke holes through the edges and tie a 7-inch string on either side. Roll the strings between your thumb and fingers to whirl your pictures.

"I'm done already!" Cards

Productive time-fillers for those who finish first.

Hanging Bug Cage

May

Catch a super bug or beetle and display it for everyone to see. Take a jelly jar and poke air holes in the top. Tie a piece of cord under the rim. Now take 3 pieces of cord 8 inches longer than the height of the jar. Tie them as shown.

Photo Mobile

May

Carefully cut the plastic rings used in packaging soda pop apart. Color the rings with permanent felt-tip markers which show through the plastic. Sandwich photos between two rings and glue them together. Hang like any mobile.

staple rings together

Photo

Rubber Cement Resist

May

Draw a design on watercolor paper with rubber cement. Let it dry. Watercolor over the rubber cement, covering the entire sheet of paper. When your painting is completely dry, carefully rub away the rubber cement.

Wall Bank

May

Make a wall bank from a liver container and a styrofoam meat tray. Clean them out thoroughly. Decorate the liver container as desired. Trace around it onto a styrofoam meat tray. Cut the styrofoam with a tab on top to hang the bank.

Glue the liver container to the styrofoam.

Liver Container

Styrofoam Meat Tray